The Theoretical Foundations of Ethics, Law, & Civil Society

The Theoretical Foundations of Ethics, Law, & Civil Society: A Primer

Edited by D. J. Murphy, Ph.D.

11th Dimension Press
Toronto, Canada

With special thanks to Professor Jeff Mitchserling

Original cover art by Robert Murphy

First Printing, 2013
ISBN 978-0-9881195-1-2

1st Dimension Books
An Imprint of 11th Dimension Press

www.11thDimensionPress.com

Table of Contents

Introduction

The purpose of this book is simple: to provide students who are not necessarily inclined to study philosophy an accessible and concise anthology of texts drawn from some of the most important and influential works on the subject of ethics generally conceived. The practical purpose of the book is to provide sufficient theoretical material to support a diverse practical and applied ethics curriculum. Accordingly, this book does not provide a comprehensive collection of texts. Rather, it provides just enough theoretical material to support sufficiently theoretical explorations of a variety of very practical ethical concerns. This book is directed at students of business, medicine, research, law, practitioners of every sort. In short this book is directed at students who are not philosophers by trade or by choice, yet who encounter genuinely philosophical and ethical challenges every day in their professional practice.

In keeping with these aspirations the book offers selections from some of the most influential authors throughout history, including Plato on moral absolutism, Aristotele on teleological ethics, Hobbes on ethical egoism, Kant on deontolgy, Locke on social contractarianism, and Bentham and Mill on utilitarianism. Except for the most general theoretical discussions addressing commerce, labour, property, and other issues relevant to the subject of justice within society (I refer here to excerpts from Smith, Locke, Marx, and the like), the book contains no topical material. That is, it does not offer discussions concerning particular topics encountered in specific areas of applied ethics. You will not find discussions explicitly addressing issues like the ethics of euthanasia, abortion, intellectual property, monopolies, censorship, prostitution, or issues of this sort. Rather, in these pages the reader will encounter the ideas, theories, and problems that have historically shaped legislation and the prevailing ethical positions with respect to such important issues.

Nor does this anthology contain any complete texts. On the contrary, when compiling this collection I took great pains to edit down the excerpts to the bare minimum necessary to convey concise understanding of the key idea presented in each text. Readers who are already familiar with the works represented here will recognize the extent to which the selections have been abridged. This is, again, in keeping with the stated purpose of this collection. One might think of what is offered here as the 'executive summary' and readers should appreciate that what has been included is, in most cases, a mere taste of a much larger work. For that reason, readers are strongly encouraged to find a more complete version of any text they find of particular interest.

Furthermore, the excerpts in this collection have been edited slightly for the sake of accessibility and readability. Although the somewhat archaic English of Hobbes remains, on a number of occasions more contemporary phrases have been substituted for old-fashioned terms. Abbreviations have been replaced with the full names of words they are meant to shorten (e.g., the abbreviations of the Biblical texts in the selection from the Summa Theologica *have been replaced with their full names). Also, certain parenthetical information or statements have been omitted. Always the justification for such modifications has been accessibility for readers not accustomed to reading philosophical texts.*

Finally, it should be mentioned that the selections are organized in chronological order. This means that readers using this book for courses organized around specific topics (as applied ethics course most often are) may find themselves bouncing from place to place through the text. Be that as it may, I settled upon a chronological ordering of the texts for two main reasons: (1) it is impossible to anticipate the variety of topics in relation to which each of the selections might be read, and (2) the chronological ordering of the selections should prevent students from mixing up the temporal order of the various discussions.

ONE

Plato

Plato (427 - 347 B.C.E) is arguably the greatest thinker of all time. He wrote and taught, for the most part, in ancient Athens, but his advice and counsel was sought by leaders of his day throughout the Hellenized world. Plato was the founder of the Academy, what some call the first university, an institution that survived some 900 years before it was finally closed by the Emperor Justinian in 529 C.E. The influence of the Academy, the ideals it was founded upon, and the many (sometimes conflicting) philosophies taught within its walls, are still prevalent today, a true testament to the endurance and greatness of Plato's thought.

Unlike later thinkers who will attempt to answer the more practical question, "How should one act if one wants to be ethical?", Plato poses the question, "What is the measure according to which an act might be judged ethical or not?" The difference between the two questions is subtle but important. It boils down to this: Plato wants to know what it is that makes an act good or bad so that he, and the rest of society, can accurately judge the goodness or badness of an action. From Plato's point of view, it's impossible to figure out how one might act ethically if we do not know what it is that makes our actions ethical. This line of thinking leads Plato to ask questions like, "What is piety?", "Why are some acts good and others bad?", and "What is justice?" These are all questions that seek to define the essence of some ultimate standard by which the goodness or badness of human actions and institutions might be judged.

In the selections compiled here we find Plato exploring these very questions. In Euthyphro, *Plato asks the questions, "What is piety?" and "What makes an action pious?" In a modern context this is equivalent to asking the question, "Where do our ethical standards come from?" Some of the answers Plato considers are still embraced today under the guise of "divine command theory" and "social contract theory", to name just two modern incarnations of Plato's ideas. Later, in selections from* Republic, *Plato assesses an opinion that is often espoused today--namely, that might makes right. He will then proceed to consider a question of the utmost importance to contemporary liberalism: "Are actions performed in private immune to ethical considerations?"*

Before proceeding is important to understand that Plato wrote in dialogue form; his work sometimes reads like the script of a play. He did so partly to illustrate the dialectical nature of his philosophy and partly to ensure the accessibility of his thinking. This format, and Plato's playful style in general, sometimes leaves his audience unsure of the position he seeks to support. For this reason it is important to note that it is generally accepted that Socrates speaks the views Plato seeks to support. That said, Plato is often ambiguous with respect to his own views and often leaves difficult questions unanswered.

Plato's Euthyphro
Where Do Ethics Come From?

SOCRATES: And what is your suit, Euthyphro? are you the pursuer or the defendant?

EUTHYPHRO: I am the pursuer.

SOCRATES: Of whom?

EUTHYPHRO: You will think me mad when I tell you.

SOCRATES: Why, has the fugitive wings?

EUTHYPHRO: Nay, he is not very volatile at his time of life.

SOCRATES: Who is he?

EUTHYPHRO: My father.

SOCRATES: Your father! my good man?

EUTHYPHRO: Yes.

SOCRATES: And of what is he accused?

EUTHYPHRO: Of murder, Socrates.

SOCRATES: By the powers, Euthyphro! how little does the common herd know of the nature of right and truth. A man must be an extraordinary man, and have made great strides in wisdom, before he could have seen his way to bring such an action.

EUTHYPHRO: Indeed, Socrates, he must.

SOCRATES: I suppose that the man whom your father murdered was one of your relatives--clearly he was; for if he had been a stranger you would never have thought of prosecuting him.

EUTHYPHRO: I am amused, Socrates, at your making a distinction between one who is a relation and one who is not a relation; for surely the pollution is the same in either case, if you knowingly associate with the murderer when you ought to clear yourself and him by proceeding against him. The real question is whether the murdered man has been justly slain. If justly, then your duty is to let the matter alone; but if unjustly, then even if the murderer lives under the same roof with you and eats at the same table, proceed against him. Now the man who is dead was a poor dependant of mine who worked for us as a field labourer on our farm in Naxos, and one day in a fit of drunken passion he got into a quarrel with one of our domestic servants and slew him. My father bound him hand and foot and threw him into a ditch, and then sent to Athens to ask of a diviner what he should do with him. Meanwhile he never attended to him and took no care about him, for he regarded him as a murderer; and thought that no great harm would be done even if he did die. Now this was just what happened. For such was the effect of cold and hunger and chains upon him, that before the messenger returned from the diviner, he was dead. And my father and family are angry with me for taking the part of the murderer and prosecuting my father. They say that he did not kill him, and that if he did, the dead man was but a murderer, and I ought not to take any notice, for that a son is impious who prosecutes a father. Which shows, Socrates, how little they know what the gods think about piety and impiety.

SOCRATES: Good heavens, Euthyphro! and is your knowledge of religion and of things pious and impious so very exact, that, supposing the circumstances to be as you state them, you are not afraid lest you too may be doing an impious thing in bringing an action against your father?

EUTHYPHRO: The best of Euthyphro, and that which distinguishes him, Socrates, from other men, is his exact knowledge of all such matters. What should I be good for without it?

SOCRATES: Rare friend! I think that I cannot do better than be your disciple. Then before the trial with Meletus comes on I shall challenge him, and say that I have always had a great interest in religious questions, and now, as he charges me with rash imaginations and innovations in religion, I have become your disciple. You, Meletus, as I shall say to him, acknowledge Euthyphro to be a great theologian, and sound in his opinions; and if you approve of him you ought to approve of me, and not have me into court; but if you disapprove, you should begin by indicting him who is my teacher, and who will be the ruin, not of the young, but of the old; that is to say, of myself whom he instructs, and of his old father whom he admonishes and chastises. And if Meletus refuses to listen to me, but will go on, and will not shift the indictment from me to you, I cannot do better than repeat this challenge in the court.

EUTHYPHRO: Yes, indeed, Socrates; and if he attempts to indict me I am mistaken if I do not find a flaw in him; the court shall have a great deal more to say to him than to me.

SOCRATES: And I, my dear friend, knowing this, am desirous of becoming your disciple. For I observe that no one appears to notice you--not even this Meletus; but his sharp eyes have found me out at once, and he has indicted me for impiety. And therefore, I adjure you to tell me the nature of piety and impiety, which you said that you knew so well, and of murder, and of other offences against the gods. What are they? Is not piety in every action always the same? and impiety, again--is it not always the opposite of piety, and also the same with itself, having, as impiety, one notion which includes whatever is impious?

EUTHYPHRO: To be sure, Socrates.

SOCRATES: And what is piety, and what is impiety?

EUTHYPHRO: Piety is doing as I am doing; that is to say, prosecuting any one who is guilty of murder, sacrilege, or of any similar crime--whether he be your father or mother, or whoever he may be--that makes no difference; and not to prosecute them is impiety. And please to consider, Socrates, what a notable proof I will give you of the truth of my words, a proof which I have already given to others:--of the principle, I mean, that the impious, whoever he may be, ought not to go unpunished. For do not men regard Zeus as the best and most righteous of the gods?--and yet they admit that he bound his father (Cronos) because he wickedly devoured his sons, and that he too had punished his own father (Uranus) for a similar reason, in a nameless manner. And yet when I proceed against my father, they are angry with me. So inconsistent are they in their way of talking when the gods are concerned, and when I am concerned.

SOCRATES: May not this be the reason, Euthyphro, why I am charged with impiety--that I cannot away with these stories about the gods? and therefore I suppose that people think me wrong. But, as you who are well informed about them approve of them, I cannot do better than assent to your superior wisdom. What else can I say, confessing as I do, that I know nothing about them? Tell me, for the love of Zeus, whether you really believe that they are true.

EUTHYPHRO: Yes, Socrates; and things more wonderful still, of which the world is in ignorance.

SOCRATES: And do you really believe that the gods fought with one another, and had dire quarrels, battles, and the like, as the poets say, and as you may see represented in the works of great artists? The temples are full of them; and notably the robe of Athene, which is carried up to the Acropolis at the great Panathenaea, is embroidered with them. Are all these tales of the gods true, Euthyphro?

EUTHYPHRO: Yes, Socrates; and, as I was saying, I can tell you, if you would like to hear them, many other things about the gods which would quite amaze you.

SOCRATES: I dare say; and you shall tell me them at some other time when I have leisure. But just at present I would rather hear from you a more precise answer, which you have not as yet given, my friend, to the question, What is 'piety'? When asked, you only replied, Doing as you do, charging your father with murder.

EUTHYPHRO: And what I said was true, Socrates.

SOCRATES: No doubt, Euthyphro; but you would admit that there are many other pious acts?

EUTHYPHRO: There are.

SOCRATES: Remember that I did not ask you to give me two or three examples of piety, but to explain the general idea which makes all pious things to be pious. Do you not recollect that there was one idea which made the impious impious, and the pious pious?

EUTHYPHRO: I remember.

SOCRATES: Tell me what is the nature of this idea, and then I shall have a standard to which I may look, and by which I may measure actions, whether yours or those of any one else, and then I shall be able to say that such and such an action is pious, such another impious.

EUTHYPHRO: I will tell you, if you like.

SOCRATES: I should very much like.

EUTHYPHRO: Piety, then, is that which is dear to the gods, and impiety is that which is not dear to them.

SOCRATES: Very good, Euthyphro; you have now given me the sort of answer which I wanted. But whether what you say is true or not I cannot as yet tell, although I make no doubt that you will prove the truth of your words.

EUTHYPHRO: Of course.

SOCRATES: Come, then, and let us examine what we are saying. That thing or person which is dear to the gods is pious, and that thing or person which is hateful to the gods is impious, these two being the extreme opposites of one another. Was not that said?

EUTHYPHRO: It was.

SOCRATES: And well said?

EUTHYPHRO: Yes, Socrates, I thought so; it was certainly said.

SOCRATES: And further, Euthyphro, the gods were admitted to have enmities and hatreds and differences?

EUTHYPHRO: Yes, that was also said.

SOCRATES: And what sort of difference creates enmity and anger? Suppose for example that you and I, my good friend, differ about a number; do differences of this sort make us enemies and set us at variance with one another? Do we not go at once to arithmetic, and put an end to them by a sum?

EUTHYPHRO: True.

SOCRATES: Or suppose that we differ about magnitudes, do we not quickly end the differences by measuring?

EUTHYPHRO: Very true.

SOCRATES: And we end a controversy about heavy and light by resorting to a weighing machine?

EUTHYPHRO: To be sure.

SOCRATES: But what differences are there which cannot be thus decided, and which therefore make us angry and set us at enmity with one another? I dare say the answer does not occur to you at the moment, and therefore I will suggest that these enmities arise when the matters of difference are the just and unjust, good and evil, honourable and dishonourable. Are not these the points about which men differ, and about which when we are unable satisfactorily to decide our differences, you and I and all of us quarrel, when we do quarrel? (Compare Alcib.)

EUTHYPHRO: Yes, Socrates, the nature of the differences about which we quarrel is such as you describe.

SOCRATES: And the quarrels of the gods, noble Euthyphro, when they occur, are of a like nature?

EUTHYPHRO: Certainly they are.

SOCRATES: They have differences of opinion, as you say, about good and evil, just and unjust, honourable and dishonourable: there would have been no quarrels among them, if there had been no such differences--would there now?

EUTHYPHRO: You are quite right.

SOCRATES: Does not every man love that which he deems noble and just and good, and hate the opposite of them?

EUTHYPHRO: Very true.

SOCRATES: But, as you say, people regard the same things, some as just and others as unjust,--about these they dispute; and so there arise wars and fightings among them.

EUTHYPHRO: Very true.

SOCRATES: Then the same things are hated by the gods and loved by the gods, and are both hateful and dear to them?

EUTHYPHRO: True.

SOCRATES: And upon this view the same things, Euthyphro, will be pious and also impious?

EUTHYPHRO: So I should suppose.

SOCRATES: Then, my friend, I remark with surprise that you have not answered the question which I asked. For I certainly did not ask you to tell me what action is both pious and impious: but now it would seem that what is loved by the gods is also hated by them. And therefore, Euthyphro, in thus chastising your father you may very likely be doing what is agreeable to Zeus but disagreeable to Cronos or Uranus, and what is acceptable to Hephaestus but unacceptable to Here, and there may be other gods who have similar differences of opinion.

EUTHYPHRO: But I believe, Socrates, that all the gods would be agreed as to the propriety of punishing a murderer: there would be no difference of opinion about that.

SOCRATES: Well, but speaking of men, Euthyphro, did you ever hear any one arguing that a murderer or any sort of evil-doer ought to be let off?

EUTHYPHRO: I should rather say that these are the questions which they are always arguing, especially in courts of law: they commit all sorts of crimes, and there is nothing which they will not do or say in their own defense.

SOCRATES: But do they admit their guilt, Euthyphro, and yet say that they ought not to be punished?

EUTHYPHRO: No; they do not.

SOCRATES: Then there are some things which they do not venture to say and do: for they do not venture to argue that the guilty are to be unpunished, but they deny their guilt, do they not?

EUTHYPHRO: Yes.

SOCRATES: Then they do not argue that the evil-doer should not be punished, but they argue about the fact of who the evil-doer is, and what he did and when?

EUTHYPHRO: True.

SOCRATES: And the gods are in the same case, if as you assert they quarrel about just and unjust, and some of them say while others deny that injustice is done among them. For surely neither God nor man will ever venture to say that the doer of injustice is not to be punished?

EUTHYPHRO: That is true, Socrates, in the main.

SOCRATES: But they join issue about the particulars--gods and men alike; and, if they dispute at all, they dispute about some act which is called in question, and which by some is affirmed to be just, by others to be unjust. Is not that true?

EUTHYPHRO: Quite true.

SOCRATES: Well then, my dear friend Euthyphro, do tell me, for my better instruction and information, what proof have you that in the opinion of all the gods a servant who is guilty of murder, and is put in chains by the master of the dead man, and dies because he is put in chains before he who bound him can learn from the interpreters of the gods what he ought to do with him, dies unjustly; and that on behalf of such an one a son ought to proceed against his father and accuse him of murder. How would you show that all the gods absolutely agree in approving of his act? Prove to me that they do, and I will applaud your wisdom as long as I live.

EUTHYPHRO: It will be a difficult task; but I could make the matter very clear indeed to you.

SOCRATES: I understand; you mean to say that I am not so quick of apprehension as the judges: for to them you will be sure to prove that the act is unjust, and hateful to the gods.

EUTHYPHRO: Yes indeed, Socrates; at least if they will listen to me.

SOCRATES: But they will be sure to listen if they find that you are a good speaker. There was a notion that came into my mind while you were speaking; I said to myself: 'Well, and what if Euthyphro does prove to me that all the gods regarded the death of the serf as unjust, how do I know anything more of the nature of piety and impiety? for granting that this action may be hateful to the gods, still piety and impiety are not adequately defined by these distinctions, for that which is hateful to the gods has been shown to be also pleasing and dear to them.' And therefore, Euthyphro, I do not ask you to prove this; I will suppose, if you like, that all the gods condemn and abominate such an action. But I will amend the definition so far as to say that what all the gods hate is impious, and what they love pious or holy; and what some of them love and others hate is both or neither. Shall this be our definition of piety and impiety?

EUTHYPHRO: Why not, Socrates?

SOCRATES: Why not! certainly, as far as I am concerned, Euthyphro, there is no reason why not. But whether this admission will greatly assist you in the task of instructing me as you promised, is a matter for you to consider.

EUTHYPHRO: Yes, I should say that what all the gods love is pious and holy, and the opposite which they all hate, impious.

SOCRATES: Ought we to enquire into the truth of this, Euthyphro, or simply to accept the mere statement on our own authority and that of others? What do you say?

EUTHYPHRO: We should enquire; and I believe that the statement will stand the test of enquiry.

SOCRATES: We shall know better, my good friend, in a little while. The point which I should first wish to understand is whether the pious or holy is beloved by the gods because it is holy, or holy because it is beloved of the gods.

EUTHYPHRO: I do not understand your meaning, Socrates.

SOCRATES: I will endeavour to explain: we, speak of carrying and we speak of being carried, of leading and being led, seeing and being seen. You know that in all such cases there is a difference, and you know also in what the difference lies?

EUTHYPHRO: I think that I understand.

SOCRATES: And is not that which is beloved distinct from that which loves?

EUTHYPHRO: Certainly.

SOCRATES: Well; and now tell me, is that which is carried in this state of carrying because it is carried, or for some other reason?

EUTHYPHRO: No; that is the reason.

SOCRATES: And the same is true of what is led and of what is seen?

EUTHYPHRO: True.

SOCRATES: And a thing is not seen because it is visible, but conversely, visible because it is seen; nor is a thing led because it is in the state of being led, or carried because it is in the state of being carried, but the converse of this. And now I think, Euthyphro, that my meaning will be intelligible; and my meaning is, that any state of action or passion implies previous action or passion. It does not become because it is becoming, but it is in a state of becoming because it becomes; neither does it suffer because it is in a state of suffering, but it is in a state of suffering because it suffers. Do you not agree?

EUTHYPHRO: Yes.

SOCRATES: Is not that which is loved in some state either of becoming or suffering?

EUTHYPHRO: Yes.

SOCRATES: And the same holds as in the previous instances; the state of being loved follows the act of being loved, and not the act the state.

EUTHYPHRO: Certainly.

SOCRATES: And what do you say of piety,

EUTHYPHRO: Is not piety, according to your definition, loved by all the gods?

EUTHYPHRO: Yes.

SOCRATES: Because it is pious or holy, or for some other reason?

EUTHYPHRO: No, that is the reason.

SOCRATES: It is loved because it is holy, not holy because it is loved?

EUTHYPHRO: Yes.

SOCRATES: And that which is dear to the gods is loved by them, and is in a state to be loved of them because it is loved of them?

EUTHYPHRO: Certainly.

SOCRATES: Then that which is dear to the gods, Euthyphro, is not holy, nor is that which is holy loved of God, as you affirm; but they are two different things.

EUTHYPHRO: How do you mean, Socrates?

SOCRATES: I mean to say that the holy has been acknowledged by us to be loved of God because it is holy, not to be holy because it is loved.

EUTHYPHRO: Yes.

SOCRATES: But that which is dear to the gods is dear to them because it is loved by them, not loved by them because it is dear to them.

EUTHYPHRO: True.

SOCRATES: But, friend Euthyphro, if that which is holy is the same with that which is dear to God, and is loved because it is holy, then that which is dear to God would have been loved as being dear to God; but if that which is dear to God is dear to him because loved by him, then that which is holy would have been holy because loved by him. But now you see that the reverse is the case, and that they are quite different from one another. For one is of a kind to be loved cause it is loved, and the other is loved because it is of a kind to be loved. Thus you appear to me, Euthyphro, when I ask you what is the essence of holiness, to offer an attribute only, and not the essence--the attribute of being loved by all the gods. But you still refuse to explain to me the nature of holiness. And therefore, if you please, I will ask you not to hide your treasure, but to tell me once more what holiness or piety really is, whether dear to the gods or not (for that is a matter about which we will not quarrel); and what is impiety?...

Plato's Republic
Does Might Make Right?

Let me first understand you, I replied. Justice, as you say, is the interest of the stronger. What, Thrasymachus, is the meaning of this? You cannot mean to say that because Polydamas, the wrestler, is stronger than we are, and finds the eating of beef conducive to his bodily strength, that to eat beef is therefore equally for our good who are weaker than he is, and right and just for us?

That's abominable of you, Socrates; you take the words in the sense which is most damaging to the argument.

Not at all, my good sir, I said; I am trying to understand them; and I wish that you would be a little clearer.

Well, he said, have you never heard that forms of government differ; there are tyrannies, and there are democracies, and there are aristocracies?

Yes, I know.

And the government is the ruling power in each state?

Certainly.

And the different forms of government make laws democratical, aristocratical, tyrannical, with a view to their several interests; and these laws, which are made by them for their own interests, are the justice which they deliver to their subjects, and him who transgresses them they punish as a breaker of the law, and unjust. And that is what I mean when I say that in all states there is the same principle of justice, which is the interest of the government; and as the government must be supposed to have power, the only reasonable conclusion is, that everywhere there is one principle of justice, which is the interest of the stronger.

Now I understand you, I said; and whether you are right or not I will try to discover. But let me remark, that in defining justice you have yourself used the word 'interest' which you forbade me to use.

It is true, however, that in your definition the words 'of the stronger' are added.

A small addition, you must allow, he said.

Great or small, never mind about that: we must first enquire whether what you are saying is the truth. Now we are both agreed that justice is interest of some sort, but you go on to say 'of the stronger'; about this addition I am not so sure, and must therefore consider further.

Proceed.

I will; and first tell me, Do you admit that it is just for subjects to obey their rulers?

I do.

But are the rulers of states absolutely infallible, or are they sometimes liable to err?

To be sure, he replied, they are liable to err.

Then in making their laws they may sometimes make them rightly, and sometimes not?

True.

When they make them rightly, they make them agreeably to their interest; when they are mistaken, contrary to their interest; you admit that?

Yes.

And the laws which they make must be obeyed by their subjects, and that is what you call justice?

Doubtless.

Then justice, according to your argument, is not only obedience to the interest of the stronger but the reverse?

What is that you are saying? he asked.

I am only repeating what you are saying, I believe. But let us consider: Have we not admitted that the rulers may be mistaken about their own interest in what they command, and also that to obey them is justice? Has not that been admitted?

Yes.

Then you must also have acknowledged justice not to be for the interest of the stronger, when the rulers unintentionally command things to be done which are to their own injury. For if, as you say, justice is the obedience which the subject renders to their commands, in that case, O wisest of men, is there any escape from the conclusion that the weaker are commanded to do, not what is for the interest, but what is for the injury of the stronger?

Nothing can be clearer, Socrates, said Polemarchus.

Yes, said Cleitophon, interposing, if you are allowed to be his witness.

But there is no need of any witness, said Polemarchus, for Thrasymachus himself acknowledges that rulers may sometimes command what is not for their own interest, and that for subjects to obey them is justice.

Yes, Polemarchus, Thrasymachus said that for subjects to do what was commanded by their rulers is just.

Yes, Cleitophon, but he also said that justice is the interest of the stronger, and, while admitting both these propositions, he further acknowledged that the stronger may command the weaker who are his subjects to do what is not for his own interest; whence follows that justice is the injury quite as much as the interest of the stronger.

But, said Cleitophon, he meant by the interest of the stronger what the stronger thought to be his interest, this was what the weaker had to do; and this was affirmed by him to be justice.

Those were not his words, rejoined Polemarchus.

Never mind, I replied, if he now says that they are, let us accept his statement. Tell me, Thrasymachus, I said, did you mean by justice what the stronger thought to be his interest, whether really so or not?

Certainly not, he said. Do you suppose that I call him who is mistaken the stronger at the time when he is mistaken?

Yes, I said, my impression was that you did so, when you admitted that the ruler was not infallible but might be sometimes mistaken.

You argue like an informer, Socrates. Do you mean, for example, that he who is mistaken about the sick is a physician in that he is mistaken? or that he who errs in arithmetic or grammar is an arithmetician or grammarian at the time when he is making the mistake, in respect of the mistake? True, we say that the physician or arithmetician or grammarian has made a mistake, but this is only a way of speaking; for the fact is that neither the grammarian nor any other person of skill ever makes a mistake in so far as he is what his name implies; they none of them err unless their skill fails them, and then they cease to be skilled artists. No artist or sage or ruler errs at the time when he is what his name implies; though he is commonly said to err, and I adopted the common mode of speaking. But to be perfectly accurate, since you are such a lover of accuracy, we should say that the ruler, in so far as he is a ruler, is unerring, and, being unerring, always commands that which is for his own interest; and the subject is required to execute his commands; and therefore, as I said at first and now repeat, justice is the interest of the stronger.

Indeed, Thrasymachus, and do I really appear to you to argue like an informer?

Certainly, he replied.

And do you suppose that I ask these questions with any design of injuring you in the argument?

Nay, he replied, 'suppose' is not the word I know it; but you will be found out, and by sheer force of argument you will never prevail.

I shall not make the attempt, my dear man; but to avoid any misunderstanding occurring between us in future, let me ask, in what sense do you speak of a ruler or stronger whose interest, as you were saying, he being the superior, it is just that the inferior should execute is he a ruler in the popular or in the strict sense of the term?

In the strictest of all senses, he said. And now cheat and play the informer if you can; I ask no quarter at your hands. But you never will be able, never.

And do you imagine, I said, that I am such a madman as to try and cheat, Thrasymachus? I might as well shave a lion.

Why, he said, you made the attempt a minute ago, and you failed.

Enough, I said, of these civilities. It will be better that I should ask you a question: Is the physician, taken in that strict sense of which you are speaking, a healer of the sick or a maker of money? And remember that I am now speaking of the true physician.

A healer of the sick, he replied.

And the pilot that is to say, the true pilot is he a captain of sailors or a mere sailor?

A captain of sailors.

The circumstance that he sails in the ship is not to be taken into account; neither is he to be called a sailor; the name pilot by which he is distinguished has nothing to do with sailing, but is significant of his skill and of his authority over the sailors.

Very true, he said.

Now, I said, every art has an interest?

Certainly.

For which the art has to consider and provide?

Yes, that is the aim of art.

And the interest of any art is the perfection of it this and nothing else?

What do you mean?

I mean what I may illustrate negatively by the example of the body. Suppose you were to ask me whether the body is self-sufficing or has wants, I should reply: Certainly the body has wants; for the body may be ill and require to be cured, and has therefore interests to which the art of medicine ministers; and this is the origin and intention of medicine, as you will acknowledge. Am I not right?

Quite right, he replied.

But is the art of medicine or any other art faulty or deficient in any quality in the same way that the eye may be deficient in sight or the ear fail of hearing, and therefore requires another art to provide for the interests of seeing and hearing has art in itself, I say, any similar liability to fault or defect, and does every art require another supplementary art to provide for its interests, and that another and another without end? Or have the arts to look only after their own interests? Or have they no need either of themselves or of another? having no faults or defects, they have no need to correct them, either by the exercise of their own art or of any other; they have only to consider the interest of their subject-matter. For every art remains pure and faultless while remaining true that is to say, while perfect and unimpaired. Take the words in your precise sense, and tell me whether I am not right.

Yes, clearly.

Then medicine does not consider the interest of medicine, but the interest of the body?

True, he said.

Nor does the art of horsemanship consider the interests of the art of horsemanship, but the interests of the horse; neither do any other arts care for themselves, for they have no needs; they care only for that which is the subject of their art?

True, he said.

But surely, Thrasymachus, the arts are the superiors and rulers of their own subjects?

To this he assented with a good deal of reluctance.

Then, I said, no science or art considers or enjoins the interest of the stronger or superior, but only the interest of the subject and weaker?

He made an attempt to contest this proposition also, but finally acquiesced.

Then, I continued, no physician, in so far as he is a physician, considers his own good in what he prescribes, but the good of his patient; for the true physician is also a ruler having the human body as a subject, and is not a mere money-maker; that has been admitted?

Yes.

And the pilot likewise, in the strict sense of the term, is a ruler of sailors and not a mere sailor?

That has been admitted.

And such a pilot and ruler will provide and prescribe for the interest of the sailor who is under him, and not for his own or the ruler's interest?

He gave a reluctant 'Yes.'

Then, I said, Thrasymachus, there is no one in any rule who, in so far as he is a ruler, considers or enjoins what is for his own interest, but always what is for the interest of his subject or suitable to his art; to that he looks, and that alone he considers in everything which he says and does.

When we had got to this point in the argument, and every one saw that the definition of justice had been completely upset, Thrasymachus, instead of replying to me, said: Tell me, Socrates, have you got a nurse?

Why do you ask such a question, I said, when you ought rather to be answering?

Because she leaves you to snivel, and never wipes your nose: she has not even taught you to know the shepherd from the sheep.

What makes you say that? I replied.

Because you fancy that the shepherd or cowherd fattens or tends the sheep or oxen with a view to their own good and not to the good of himself or his master; and you further imagine that the rulers of states, if they are true rulers, never think of their subjects as sheep, and that they are not studying their own advantage day and night. Oh, no; and so entirely astray are you in your ideas about the just and unjust as not even to know that justice and the just are in reality another's good; that is to say, the interest of the ruler and stronger, and the loss of the subject and servant; and injustice the opposite; for the unjust is lord over the truly simple and just: he is the stronger, and his subjects do what is for his interest, and minister to his happiness, which is very far from being their own. Consider further, most foolish Socrates, that the just is always a loser in comparison with the unjust. First of all, in private contracts: wherever the unjust is the partner of the just you will find that, when the partnership is dissolved, the unjust man has always more and the just less. Secondly, in their dealings with the State: when there is an income-tax, the just man will pay more and the unjust less on the same amount of income; and when there is anything to be received the one gains nothing and the other much. Observe also what happens when they take an office; there is the just man neglecting his affairs and perhaps suffering other losses, and getting nothing out of the public, because he is just; moreover he is hated by his friends and acquaintance for refusing to serve them in unlawful ways. But all this is reversed in the case of the unjust man. I am speaking, as before, of injustice on a large scale in which the advantage of the unjust is most apparent; and my meaning will be most clearly seen if we turn to that highest form of injustice in which the criminal is the happiest of men, and the sufferers or those who refuse to do injustice are the most miserable that is to say tyranny, which by fraud and force takes away the property of others, not little by little but wholesale; comprehending in one, things sacred as well as profane, private and public; for which acts of wrong, if he were detected perpetrating any one of them singly, he would be punished and incur great disgrace they who do such wrong in particular cases are called robbers of temples, and man-stealers and burglars and swindlers and thieves. But when a man besides taking away the money of the citizens has made slaves of them, then, instead of these names of reproach, he is termed happy and blessed, not only by the citizens but by all who hear of his having achieved the consummation of injustice. For mankind censure injustice, fearing that they may be the victims of it and not because they shrink from committing it. And thus, as I have shown, Socrates, injustice, when on a sufficient scale, has more strength and freedom and mastery than justice; and, as I said at first, justice is the interest of the stronger, whereas injustice is a man's own profit and interest...

Plato's Republic
The Myth of Gyges

They say that to do injustice is, by nature, good; to suffer injustice, evil; but that the evil is greater than the good. And so when men have both done and suffered injustice and have had experience of both, not being able to avoid the one and obtain the other, they think that they had better agree among themselves to have neither; hence there arise laws and mutual covenants; and that which is ordained by law is termed by them lawful and just. This they affirm to be the origin and nature of justice; it is a mean or compromise, between the best of all, which is to do injustice and not be punished, and the worst of all, which is to suffer injustice without the power of retaliation; and justice, being at a middle point between the two, is tolerated not as a good, but as the lesser evil, and honoured by reason of the inability of men to do injustice. For no man who is worthy to be called a man would ever submit to such an agreement if he were able to resist; he would be mad if he did. Such is the received account, Socrates, of the nature and origin of justice.

Now that those who practice justice do so involuntarily and because they have not the power to be unjust will best appear if we imagine something of this kind: having given both to the just and the unjust power to do what they will, let us watch and see whither desire will lead them; then we shall discover in the very act the just and unjust man to be proceeding along the same road, following their interest, which all natures deem to be their good, and are only diverted into the path of justice by the force of law. The liberty which we are supposing may be most completely given to them in the form of such a power as is said to have been possessed by Gyges, the ancestor of Croesus the Lydian.

According to the tradition, Gyges was a shepherd in the service of the king of Lydia; there was a great storm, and an earthquake made an opening in the earth at the place where he was feeding his flock. Amazed at the sight, he descended into the opening, where, among other marvels, he beheld a hollow brazen horse, having doors, at which he stooping and looking in saw a dead body of stature, as appeared to him, more than human, and having nothing on but a gold ring; this he took from the finger of the dead and reascended. Now the shepherds met together, according to custom, that they might send their monthly report about the flocks to the king; into their assembly he came having the ring on his finger, and as he was sitting among them he chanced to turn the collet of the ring inside his hand, when instantly he became invisible to the rest of the company and they began to speak of him as if he were no longer present. He was astonished at this, and again touching the ring he turned the collet outwards and reappeared; he made several trials of the ring, and always with the same result, when he turned the collet inwards he became invisible, when outwards he reappeared. Whereupon he contrived to be chosen one of the messengers who were sent to the court; whereas soon as he arrived he seduced the queen, and with her help conspired against the king and slew him, and took the kingdom. Suppose now that there were two such magic rings, and the just put on one of them and the unjust the other; no man can be imagined to be of such an iron nature that he would stand fast in justice. No man would keep his hands off what was not his own when he could safely take what he liked out of the market, or go into houses and lie with any one at his pleasure, or kill or release from prison whom he would, and in all respects be like a God among men. Then the actions of the just would be as the actions of the unjust; they would both come at last to the same point. And this we may truly affirm to be a great proof that a man is just, not willingly or because he thinks that justice is any good to him individually, but of necessity, for wherever any one thinks that he can safely be unjust, there he is unjust. For all men believe in their hearts that injustice is far more profitable to the individual than justice, and he who argues as I have been supposing, will say that they are right. If you could imagine any one obtaining this power of becoming invisible, and never doing any wrong or touching what was another's, he would be thought by the lookers-on to be a most wretched idiot, although they would praise him to one another's faces, and keep up appearances with one another from a fear that they too might suffer injustice...

Two

Aristotle

The philosopher known as Aristotle (384 - 322 B.C.E.) was born in Stagira in the Macedonian kingdom. He was the son of Nicomachus, the court physician to King Amyntas of Macedonia (grandfather to Alexander the Great) and, if his father had lived, the Stagirite, as he is sometimes called, would likely have become a medical man like his father. The boy became the ward of Proxeneus, a male relative of which very little is known, who brought the Stagirite to Athens, where he was enrolled in Plato's Academy. In the Academy the Stagirite would stand out for his superior intellectual prowess so much so that Plato himself would give him the name "Aristotle", which, roughly translated, means "superior in purpose."

Aristotle's life was full of romance and intrigue. After roughly twenty years of study at the Academy and following Plato's death, Aristotle travelled to Asia Minor, where he married the daughter of Hermias of Atarneus. However, when the Persians invaded Atarneus and crucified Hermias, Aristotle was forced to flee. On the invitation of Philip II of Macedon, Aristotle returned to Macedonia, where he became became the tutor of Philip's son Alexander (not yet "Alexander the Great") and a few of Alexander's contemporaries. In 335 B.C.E. Aristotle returned to Athens where he founded his own school, the Lyceum.

Aristotle's surviving work is very different from that of Plato. It's written in the treatise style and is thorough and systematic. Aristotle's works address a wide breadth of subject matter, from grammar to biology, economics and meteorology. In fact, what is today referred to as Aristotle's corpus is commonly believed to be the core set of texts that served as the basis for the curriculum of the Lyceum.

Three treatises on ethics are attributed to Aristotle, however, the most famous of the three is the treatise Aristotle named in honour of his father--namely, the Nicomachean Ethics. *Unlike his mentor Plato, Aristotle concerns himself with the question of how one should act. In the first selection, drawn from book one of* Nicomachean Ethics, *Aristotle articulates the foundational principle of his philosophy: "every art and every inquiry, and similarly every action and pursuit, is thought to aim at some good." According to Aristotle, a comprehensive explanation of any given object, event, action, anything at all, must take into consideration the reason for that thing's existence or the motivations behind the given event or action. This mode of explanation comes to be known as Aristotle's 'teleology' --literally, explanation (*logos*) with reference to a thing's purpose or goal (*telos*). This principle gives shape to Aristotle's ethics and his entire worldview.*

Unlike his mentor Plato, Aristotle concerns himself with the question of how one should act in oder to be ethical. In the second selection, drawn from book two of Nicomachean Ethics, *Aristotle offers what he believes to be the guiding principle that, when followed, will cultivate habits of ethical behaviour. For Aristotle, virtue, like health, is a goal to be sought after, achieved, and sustained, through constant discipline and work.*

Aristotle's Ethics

Happiness is Every Person's Goal

1 Every art and every inquiry, and similarly every action and pursuit, is thought to aim at some good; and for this reason the good has rightly been declared to be that at which all things aim. But a certain difference is found among ends; some are activities, others are products apart from the activities that produce them. Where there are ends apart from the actions, it is the nature of the products to be better than the activities. Now, as there are many actions, arts, and sciences, their ends also are many; the end of the medical art is health, that of shipbuilding a vessel, that of strategy victory, that of economics wealth. But where such arts fall under a single capacity- as bridle-making and the other arts concerned with the equipment of horses fall under the art of riding, and this and every military action under strategy, in the same way other arts fall under yet others- in all of these the ends of the master arts are to be preferred to all the subordinate ends; for it is for the sake of the former that the latter are pursued. It makes no difference whether the activities themselves are the ends of the actions, or something else apart from the activities, as in the case of the sciences just mentioned.

2 If, then, there is some end of the things we do, which we desire for its own sake (everything else being desired for the sake of this), and if we do not choose everything for the sake of something else (for at that rate the process would go on to infinity, so that our desire would be empty and vain), clearly this must be the good and the chief good. Will not the knowledge of it, then, have a great influence on life? Shall we not, like archers who have a mark to aim at, be more likely to hit upon what is right? If so, we must try, in outline at least, to determine what it is, and of which of the sciences or capacities it is the object. It would seem to belong to the most

authoritative art and that which is most truly the master art. And politics appears to be of this nature; for it is this that ordains which of the sciences should be studied in a state, and which each class of citizens should learn and up to what point they should learn them; and we see even the most highly esteemed of capacities to fall under this, e.g. strategy, economics, rhetoric; now, since politics uses the rest of the sciences, and since, again, it legislates as to what we are to do and what we are to abstain from, the end of this science must include those of the others, so that this end must be the good for man. For even if the end is the same for a single man and for a state, that of the state seems at all events something greater and more complete whether to attain or to preserve; though it is worth while to attain the end merely for one man, it is finer and more godlike to attain it for a nation or for city-states. These, then, are the ends at which our inquiry aims, since it is political science, in one sense of that term…

5 Let us, however, resume our discussion from the point at which we digressed. To judge from the lives that men lead, most men, and men of the most vulgar type, seem (not without some ground) to identify the good, or happiness, with pleasure; which is the reason why they love the life of enjoyment. For there are, we may say, three prominent types of life- that just mentioned, the political, and thirdly the contemplative life. Now the mass of mankind are evidently quite slavish in their tastes, preferring a life suitable to beasts, but they get some ground for their view from the fact that many of those in high places share the tastes of Sardanapallus. A consideration of the prominent types of life shows that people of superior refinement and of active disposition identify happiness with honour; for this is, roughly speaking, the end of the political life. But it seems too superficial to be what we are looking for, since it is thought to depend on those who bestow honour rather than on him who receives it, but the good we divine to be something proper to a man and not easily taken from him. Further, men seem to pursue honour in order that they may be assured of their goodness; at least it is by men of practical wisdom that they seek to be honoured, and among those who know them, and on the ground of their virtue; clearly, then, according to them, at any rate, virtue is better. And perhaps one might even suppose this to be, rather than honour, the end of the political life. But even this appears somewhat incomplete; for possession of virtue seems actually compatible with being asleep, or with lifelong inactivity, and, further, with the greatest sufferings and misfortunes; but a man who was living so no one would call happy, unless he were maintaining a thesis at all costs. But enough of this; for the subject has been sufficiently treated even in the current discussions. Third comes the contemplative life, which we shall consider later.

The life of money-making is one undertaken under compulsion, and wealth is evidently not the good we are seeking; for it is merely useful and for the sake of something else. And so one might rather take the aforenamed objects to be ends; for they are loved for themselves. But it is evident that not even these are ends; yet many arguments have been thrown away in support of them. Let us leave this subject, then…

Aristotle's Ethics
Virtue is a Habit of Moderation

1 Virtue, then, being of two kinds, intellectual and moral, intellectual virtue in the main owes both its birth and its growth to teaching (for which reason it requires experience and time), while moral virtue comes about as a result of habit, whence also its name (ethike) is one that is formed by a slight variation from the word ethos (habit). From this it is also plain that none of the moral virtues arises in us by nature; for nothing that exists by nature can form a habit contrary to its nature. For instance the stone which by nature moves downwards cannot be habituated to move upwards, not even if one tries to train it by throwing it up ten thousand times; nor can fire be habituated to move downwards, nor can anything else that by nature behaves in one way be trained to behave in another. Neither by nature, then, nor contrary to nature do the virtues arise in us; rather we are adapted by nature to receive them, and are made perfect by habit.

Again, of all the things that come to us by nature we first acquire the potentiality and later exhibit the activity (this is plain in the case of the senses; for it was not by often seeing or often hearing that we got these senses, but on the contrary we had them before we used them, and did not come to have them by using them); but the virtues we get by first exercising them, as also happens in the case of the arts as well. For the things we have to learn before we can do them, we learn by doing them, e.g. men become builders by building and lyre players by playing the lyre; so too we become just by doing just acts, temperate by doing temperate acts, brave by doing brave acts.

This is confirmed by what happens in states; for legislators make the citizens good by forming habits in them, and this is the wish of every legislator, and those who do not effect it miss their mark, and it is in this that a good constitution differs from a bad one.

Again, it is from the same causes and by the same means that every virtue is both produced and destroyed, and similarly every art; for it is from playing the lyre that both good and bad lyre-players are produced. And the corresponding statement is true of builders and of all the rest; men will be good or bad builders as a result of building well or badly. For if this were not so, there would have been no need of a teacher, but all men would have been born good or bad at their craft. This, then, is the case with the virtues also; by doing the acts that we do in our transactions with other men we become just or unjust, and by doing the acts that we do in the presence of danger, and being habituated to feel fear or confidence, we become brave or cowardly. The same is true of appetites and feelings of anger; some men become temperate and good-tempered, others self-indulgent and irascible, by behaving in one way or the other in the appropriate circumstances. Thus, in one word, states of character arise out of like activities. This is why the activities we exhibit must be of a certain kind; it is because the states of character correspond to the differences between these. It makes no small difference, then, whether we form habits of one kind or of another from our very youth; it makes a very great difference, or rather all the difference…

4 The question might be asked,; what we mean by saying that we must become just by doing just acts, and temperate by doing temperate acts; for if men do just and temperate acts, they are already just and temperate, exactly as, if they do what is in accordance with the laws of grammar and of music, they are grammarians and musicians.

Or is this not true even of the arts? It is possible to do something that is in accordance with the laws of grammar, either by chance or at the suggestion of another. A man will be a grammarian, then, only when he has both done something grammatical and done it grammatically; and this means doing it in accordance with the grammatical knowledge in himself.

Again, the case of the arts and that of the virtues are not similar; for the products of the arts have their goodness in themselves, so that it is enough that they should have a certain character, but if the acts that are in accordance with the virtues have themselves a certain character it does not follow that they are done justly or temperately. The agent also must be in a certain condition when he does them; in the first place he must have knowledge, secondly he must choose the acts, and choose them for their own sakes, and thirdly his action must proceed from a firm and unchangeable character.

These are not reckoned in as conditions of the possession of the arts, except the bare knowledge; but as a condition of the possession of the virtues knowledge has little or no weight, while the other conditions count not for a little but for everything, i.e. the very conditions which result from often doing just and temperate acts.

Actions, then, are called just and temperate when they are such as the just or the temperate man would do; but it is not the man who does these that is just and temperate, but the man who also does them as just and temperate men do them. It is well said, then, that it is by doing just acts that the just man is produced, and by doing temperate acts the temperate man; without doing these no one would have even a prospect of becoming good.

But most people do not do these, but take refuge in theory and think they are being philosophers and will become good in this way, behaving somewhat like patients who listen attentively to their doctors, but do none of the things they are ordered to do. As the latter will not be made well in body by such a course of treatment, the former will not be made well in soul by such a course of philosophy.

5 Next we must consider what virtue is. Since things that are found in the soul are of three kinds- passions, faculties, states of character, virtue must be one of these. By passions I mean appetite, anger, fear, confidence, envy, joy, friendly feeling, hatred, longing, emulation, pity, and in general the feelings that are accompanied by pleasure or pain; by faculties the things in virtue of which we are said to be capable of feeling these, e.g. of becoming angry or being pained or feeling pity; by states of character the things in virtue of which we stand well or badly with reference to the passions, e.g. with reference to anger we stand badly if we feel it violently or too weakly, and well if we feel it moderately; and similarly with reference to the other passions.

Now neither the virtues nor the vices are passions, because we are not called good or bad on the ground of our passions, but are so called on the ground of our virtues and our vices, and because we are neither praised nor blamed for our passions (for the man who feels fear or anger is not praised, nor is the man who simply feels anger blamed, but the man who feels it in a certain way), but for our virtues and our vices we are praised or blamed.

Again, we feel anger and fear without choice, but the virtues are modes of choice or involve choice. Further, in respect of the passions we are said to be moved, but in respect of the virtues and the vices we are said not to be moved but to be disposed in a particular way.

For these reasons also they are not faculties; for we are neither called good nor bad, nor praised nor blamed, for the simple capacity of feeling the passions; again, we have the faculties by nature, but we are not made good or bad by nature; we have spoken of this before. If, then, the virtues are neither passions nor faculties, all that remains is that they should be states of character.

Thus we have stated what virtue is in respect of its genus.

6 We must, however, not only describe virtue as a state of character, but also say what sort of state it is. We may remark, then, that every virtue or excellence both brings into good condition the thing of which it is the excellence and makes the work of that thing be done well; e.g. the excellence of the eye makes both the eye and its work good; for it is by the excellence of the eye that we see well. Similarly the excellence of the horse makes a horse both good in itself and good at running and at carrying its rider and at awaiting the attack of the enemy. Therefore, if this is true in every case, the virtue of man also will be the state of character which makes a man good and which makes him do his own work well.

How this is to happen we have stated already, but it will be made plain also by the following consideration of the specific nature of virtue. In everything that is continuous and divisible it is possible to take more, less, or an equal amount, and that either in terms of the thing itself or relatively to us; and the equal is an intermediate between excess and defect. By the intermediate in the object I mean that which is equidistant from each of the extremes, which is one and the same for all men; by the intermediate relatively to us that which is neither too much nor too little- and this is not one, nor the same for all. For instance, if ten is many and two is few, six is the intermediate, taken in terms of the object; for it exceeds and is exceeded by an equal amount; this is intermediate according to arithmetical proportion. But the intermediate relatively to us is not to be taken so; if ten pounds are too much for a particular person to eat and two too little, it does not follow that the trainer will order six pounds; for this also is perhaps too much for the person who is to take it, or too little- too little for Milo, too much for the beginner in athletic exercises. The same is true of running and wrestling. Thus a master of any art avoids excess and defect, but seeks the intermediate and chooses this- the intermediate not in the object but relatively to us.

If it is thus, then, that every art does its work well- by looking to the intermediate and judging its works by this standard (so that we often say of good works of art that it is not possible either to take away or to add anything, implying that excess and defect destroy the goodness of works of art, while the mean preserves it; and good artists, as we say, look to this in their work), and if, further, virtue is more exact and better than any art, as nature also is, then virtue must have the quality of aiming at the intermediate. I mean moral virtue; for it is this that is concerned with passions and actions, and in these there is excess, defect, and the intermediate. For instance, both fear and confidence and appetite and anger and pity and in general pleasure and pain may be felt both too much and too little, and in both cases not well; but to feel them at the right times, with reference to the right objects, towards the right people, with the right motive, and in the right way, is what is both intermediate and best, and this is characteristic of virtue. Similarly with regard to actions also there is excess, defect, and the intermediate. Now virtue is concerned with passions and actions, in which excess is a form of failure, and so is defect, while the intermediate is praised and is a form of success; and being praised and being successful are both characteristics of virtue. Therefore virtue is a kind of mean, since, as we have seen, it aims at what is intermediate.

Again, it is possible to fail in many ways (for evil belongs to the class of the unlimited, as the Pythagoreans conjectured, and good to that of the limited), while to succeed is possible only in one way (for which reason also one is easy and the other difficult- to miss the mark easy, to hit it difficult); for these reasons also, then, excess and defect are characteristic of vice, and the mean of virtue;

For men are good in but one way, but bad in many.

Virtue, then, is a state of character concerned with choice, lying in a mean, i.e. the mean relative to us, this being determined by a rational principle, and by that principle by which the man of practical wisdom would determine it. Now it is a mean between two vices, that which depends on excess and that which depends on defect; and again it is a mean because the vices respectively fall short of or exceed what is right in both passions and actions, while virtue both finds and chooses that which is intermediate. Hence in respect of its substance and the definition which states its essence virtue is a mean, with regard to what is best and right an extreme.

But not every action nor every passion admits of a mean; for some have names that already imply badness, e.g. spite, shamelessness, envy, and in the case of actions adultery, theft, murder; for all of these and suchlike things imply by their names that they are themselves bad, and not the excesses or deficiencies of them. It is not possible, then, ever to be right with regard to them; one must always be wrong. Nor does goodness or badness with regard to such things depend on committing adultery with the right woman, at the right time, and in the right way, but simply to do any of them is to go wrong. It would be equally absurd, then, to expect that in unjust, cowardly, and voluptuous action there should be a mean, an excess, and a deficiency; for at that rate there would be a mean of excess and of deficiency, an excess of excess, and a deficiency of deficiency. But as there is no excess and deficiency of temperance and courage because what is intermediate is in a sense an extreme, so too of the actions we have mentioned there is no mean nor any excess and deficiency, but however they are done they are wrong; for in general there is neither a mean of excess and deficiency, nor excess and deficiency of a mean…

THREE

Saint Thomas Aquinas

Thomas Aquinas (1225 - 1274) was born in Aquino, Sicily, then a kingdom unto itself, to a family of lesser aristocrats. As was common practice in his day, Thomas was committed by his family to a career in the Church. However, when Thomas decided to join the Dominican Order rather than become a Benedictine like his uncle, Thomas was held captive in the family castle for two years in an effort to coerce him into changing his mind.

When Thomas was released he travelled to Rome before moving on Paris, where he studied under Albertus Magnus. Magnus would eventually refer to Thomas as the "Dumb Ox" for his plodding and methodical approach to scholarship. Despite this characterization Thomas would make enduring contributions to Aristotle scholarship, law, and human rights. He is also considered one of the greatest Catholic scholars of all time.

Thomas's Summa Theologica *is considered to be the definitive compendium of Catholic philosophy. It contains Thomas's famous five ways to prove the existence of God, his statement of the general principles of morality, and his Christology, among many other extremely influential discussions.*

In the section included here we find Thomas's analysis of law, its various kinds, its numerous sources, and its source of legitimacy. These texts are the basis of what contemporary scholars, following Thomas, refer to as "Natural Law Theory." Natural Law Theory is now, and has long been, one of the dominant approaches to the analysis of law.

Thomas's style is indeed quite methodical. He will introduce each of his topics as a series of questions. He will then proceed to answer each question in a series of articles. The articles themselves open with a question followed by a series of objections to an affirmative answer to the question. It is important to understand that Aquinas's view, that is, the position he seeks to defend, is the affirmative answer to the question and NOT the objections. Aquinas begins to elaborate on his own views when he writes, "on the contrary," followed by direct responses to the objections.

Summa Theologica

Concerning the Different Kinds of Law

We must now consider the various kinds of law: under which head there are six points of inquiry:

1. Whether there is an eternal law?
2. Whether there is a natural law?
3. Whether there is a human law?
4. Whether there is a Divine law?
5. Whether there is one Divine law, or several?
6. Whether there is a law of sin?

FIRST ARTICLE

Whether There Is an Eternal Law?

Objection 1: It would seem that there is no eternal law. Because every law is imposed on someone. But there was not someone from eternity on whom a law could be imposed: since God alone was from eternity. Therefore no law is eternal.

Objection 2: Further, promulgation is essential to law. But promulgation could not be from eternity: because there was no one to whom it could be promulgated from eternity. Therefore no law can be eternal.

Objection 3: Further, a law implies order to an end. But nothing ordained to an end is eternal: for the last end alone is eternal. Therefore no law is eternal.

On the contrary, Augustine says: "That Law which is the Supreme Reason cannot be understood to be otherwise than unchangeable and eternal."

I answer that, As stated above, a law is nothing else but a dictate of practical reason emanating from the ruler who governs a perfect community. Now it is evident, granted that the world is ruled by Divine Providence, as was stated in the First Part, that the whole community of the universe is governed by Divine Reason. Wherefore the very Idea of the government of things in God the Ruler of the universe, has the nature of a law. And since the Divine Reason's conception of things is not subject to time but is eternal, according to Proverbs 8:23, therefore it is that this kind of law must be called eternal.

Reply To Objection 1: Those things that are not in themselves, exist with God, inasmuch as they are foreknown and preordained by Him, according to Romans 4:17: "Who calls those things that are not, as those that are." Accordingly the eternal concept of the Divine law bears the character of an eternal law, in so far as it is ordained by God to the government of things foreknown by Him.

Reply To Objection 2: Promulgation is made by word of mouth or in writing; and in both ways the eternal law is promulgated: because both the Divine Word and the writing of the Book of Life are eternal. But the promulgation cannot be from eternity on the part of the creature that hears or reads.

Reply To Objection 3: The law implies order to the end actively, in so far as it directs certain things to the end; but not passively—that is to say, the law itself is not ordained to the end—except accidentally, in a governor whose end is extrinsic to him, and to which end his law must needs be ordained. But the end of the Divine government is God Himself, and His law is not distinct from Himself. Wherefore the eternal law is not ordained to another end.

SECOND ARTICLE

Whether There Is in Us a Natural Law?

Objection 1: It would seem that there is no natural law in us. Because man is governed sufficiently by the eternal law: for Augustine says that "the eternal law is that by which it is right that all things should be most orderly." But nature does not abound in superfluities as neither does she fail in necessaries. Therefore no law is natural to man.

Objection 2: Further, by the law man is directed, in his acts, to the end, as stated above. But the directing of human acts to their end is not a function of nature, as is the case in irrational creatures, which act for an end solely by their natural appetite; whereas man acts for an end by his reason and will. Therefore no law is natural to man.

Objection 3: Further, the more a man is free, the less is he under the law. But man is freer than all the animals, on account of his free-will, with which he is endowed above all other animals. Since therefore other animals are not subject to a natural law, neither is man subject to a natural law.

On the contrary, A gloss on Romans 2:14: "When the Gentiles, who have not the law, do by nature those things that are of the law," comments as follows: "Although they have no written law, yet they have the natural law, whereby each one knows, and is conscious of, what is good and what is evil."

I answer that, As stated above, law, being a rule and measure, can be in a person in two ways: in one way, as in him that rules and measures; in another way, as in that which is ruled and measured, since a thing is ruled and measured, in so far as it partakes of the rule or measure. Wherefore, since all things subject to Divine providence are ruled and measured by the eternal law, as was stated above; it is evident that all things partake somewhat of the eternal law, in so far as, namely, from its being imprinted on them, they derive their respective inclinations to their proper acts and ends. Now among all others, the rational creature is subject to Divine providence in the most excellent way, in so far as it partakes of a share of providence, by being provident both for itself and for others. Wherefore it has a share of the Eternal Reason, whereby it has a natural inclination to its proper act and end: and this participation of the eternal law in the rational creature is called the natural law. Hence the Psalmist after saying (Psalms 4:6): "Offer up the sacrifice of justice," as though someone asked what the works of justice are, adds: "Many say, Who showeth us good things?" in answer to which question he says: "The light of Thy countenance, O Lord, is signed upon us": thus implying that the light of natural reason, whereby we discern what is good and what is evil, which is the function of the natural law, is nothing else than an imprint on us of the Divine light. It is therefore evident that the natural law is nothing else than the rational creature's participation of the eternal law.

Reply To Objection 1: This argument would hold, if the natural law were something different from the eternal law: whereas it is nothing but a participation thereof, as stated above.

Reply To Objection 2: Every act of reason and will in us is based on that which is according to nature, as stated above: for every act of reasoning is based on principles that are known naturally, and every act of appetite in respect of the means is derived from the natural appetite in respect of the last end. Accordingly the first direction of our acts to their end must needs be in virtue of the natural law.

Reply To Objection 3: Even irrational animals partake in their own way of the Eternal Reason, just as the rational creature does. But because the rational creature partakes thereof in an intellectual and rational manner, therefore the participation of the eternal law in the rational creature is properly called a law, since a law is something pertaining to reason, as stated above. Irrational creatures, however, do not partake thereof in a rational manner, wherefore there is no participation of the eternal law in them, except by way of similitude.

THIRD ARTICLE

Whether There Is a Human Law?

Objection 1: It would seem that there is not a human law. For the natural law is a participation of the eternal law, as stated above. Now through the eternal law "all things are most orderly," as Augustine states. Therefore the natural law suffices for the ordering of all human affairs. Consequently there is no need for a human law.

Objection 2: Further, a law bears the character of a measure, as stated above. But human reason is not a measure of things, but vice versa, as stated in Metaphysics X 5. Therefore no law can emanate from human reason.

Objection 3: Further, a measure should be most certain, as stated in Metaphysics X 3. But the dictates of human reason in matters of conduct are uncertain, according to the Wisdom of Solomon 9:14: "The thoughts of mortal men are fearful, and our counsels uncertain." Therefore no law can emanate from human reason.

On the contrary, Augustine distinguishes two kinds of law, the one eternal, the other temporal, which he calls human.

I answer that, as stated above, a law is a dictate of the practical reason. Now it is to be observed that the same procedure takes place in the practical and in the speculative reason: for each proceeds from principles to conclusions, as stated above. Accordingly we conclude that just as, in the speculative reason, from naturally known indemonstrable principles, we draw the conclusions of the various sciences, the knowledge of which is not imparted to us by nature, but acquired by the efforts of reason, so too it is from the precepts of the natural law, as from general and indemonstrable principles, that the human reason needs to proceed to the more particular determination of certain matters. These particular determinations, devised by human reason, are called human laws, provided the other essential conditions of law be observed, as stated above.

Wherefore Tully says in his Rhetoric that "justice has its source in nature; thence certain things came into custom by reason of their utility; afterwards these things which emanated from nature and were approved by custom, were sanctioned by fear and reverence for the law."

Reply To Objection 1: The human reason cannot have a full participation of the dictate of the Divine Reason, but according to its own mode, and imperfectly. Consequently, as on the part of the speculative reason, by a natural participation of Divine Wisdom, there is in us the knowledge of certain general principles, but not proper knowledge of each single truth, such as that contained in the Divine Wisdom; so too, on the part of the practical reason, man has a natural participation of the eternal law, according to certain general principles, but not as regards the particular determinations of individual cases, which are, however, contained in the eternal law. Hence the need for human reason to proceed further to sanction them by law.

Reply To Objection 2: Human reason is not, of itself, the rule of things: but the principles impressed on it by nature, are general rules and measures of all things relating to human conduct, whereof the natural reason is the rule and measure, although it is not the measure of things that are from nature.

Reply To Objection 3: The practical reason is concerned with practical matters, which are singular and contingent: but not with necessary things, with which the speculative reason is concerned. Wherefore human laws cannot have that inerrancy that belongs to the demonstrated conclusions of sciences. Nor is it necessary for every measure to be altogether unerring and certain, but according as it is possible in its own particular genus.

FOURTH ARTICLE

Whether There Was Any Need for a Divine Law?

Objection 1: It would seem that there was no need for a Divine law. Because, as stated above, the natural law is a participation in us of the eternal law. But the eternal law is a Divine law, as stated above. Therefore there was no need for a Divine law in addition to the natural law, and human laws derived therefrom.

Objection 2: Further, it is written (Ecclesiastes 15:14) that "God left man in the hand of his own counsel." Now counsel is an act of reason, as stated above. Therefore man was left to the direction of his reason. But a dictate of human reason is a human law as stated above. Therefore there is no need for man to be governed also by a Divine law.

Objection 3: Further, human nature is more self-sufficing than irrational creatures. But irrational creatures have no Divine law besides the natural inclination impressed on them. Much less, therefore, should the rational creature have a Divine law in addition to the natural law.

On the contrary, David prayed God to set His law before him, saying (Psalms. 118:33): "Set before me for a law the way of Thy justifications, O Lord."

I answer that, Besides the natural and the human law it was necessary for the directing of human conduct to have a Divine law. And this for four reasons. First, because it is by law that man is directed how to perform his proper acts in view of his last end. And indeed if man were ordained to no other end than that which is proportionate to his natural faculty, there would be no need for man to have any further direction of the part of his reason, besides the natural law and human law which is derived from it. But since man is ordained to an end of eternal happiness which is improportionate to man's natural faculty, as stated above, therefore it was necessary that, besides the natural and the human law, man should be directed to his end by a law given by God.

Secondly, because, on account of the uncertainty of human judgment, especially on contingent and particular matters, different people form different judgments on human acts; whence also different and contrary laws result. In order, therefore, that man may know without any doubt what he ought to do and what he ought to avoid, it was necessary for man to be directed in his proper acts by a law given by God, for it is certain that such a law cannot err.

Thirdly, because man can make laws in those matters of which he is competent to judge. But man is not competent to judge of interior movements, that are hidden, but only of exterior acts which appear: and yet for the perfection of virtue it is necessary for man to conduct himself aright in both kinds of acts. Consequently human law could not sufficiently curb and direct interior acts; and it was necessary for this purpose that a Divine law should supervene.

Fourthly, because, as Augustine says, human law cannot punish or forbid all evil deeds: since while aiming at doing away with all evils, it would do away with many good things, and would hinder the advance of the common good, which is necessary for human intercourse. In order, therefore, that no evil might remain unforbidden and unpunished, it was necessary for the Divine law to supervene, whereby all sins are forbidden.

And these four causes are touched upon in Psalms 118:8, where it is said: "The law of the Lord is unspotted," i.e. allowing no foulness of sin; "converting souls," because it directs not only exterior, but also interior acts; "the testimony of the Lord is faithful," because of the certainty of what is true and right; "giving wisdom to little ones," by directing man to an end supernatural and Divine.

Reply To Objection 1: By the natural law the eternal law is participated proportionately to the capacity of human nature. But to his supernatural end man needs to be directed in a yet higher way. Hence the additional law given by God, whereby man shares more perfectly in the eternal law.

Reply To Objection 2: Counsel is a kind of inquiry: hence it must proceed from some principles. Nor is it enough for it to proceed from principles imparted by nature, which are the precepts of the natural law, for the reasons given above: but there is need for certain additional principles, namely, the precepts of the Divine law.

Reply To Objection 3: Irrational creatures are not ordained to an end higher than that which is proportionate to their natural powers: consequently the comparison fails.

FIFTH ARTICLE

Whether There Is but One Divine Law?

Objection 1: It would seem that there is but one Divine law. Because, where there is one king in one kingdom there is but one law. Now the whole of mankind is compared to God as to one king, according to Psalms 46:8: "God is the King of all the earth." Therefore there is but one Divine law.

Objection 2: Further, every law is directed to the end which the lawgiver intends for those for whom he makes the law. But God intends one and the same thing for all men; since according to 1 Timothy 2:4: "He will have all men to be saved, and to come to the knowledge of the truth." Therefore there is but one Divine law.

Objection 3: Further, the Divine law seems to be more akin to the eternal law, which is one, than the natural law, according as the revelation of grace is of a higher order than natural knowledge. Therefore much more is the Divine law but one.

On the contrary, The Apostle says (Hebrews 7:12): "The priesthood being translated, it is necessary that a translation also be made of the law." But the priesthood is twofold, as stated in the same passage, viz. the levitical priesthood, and the priesthood of Christ.

Therefore the Divine law is twofold, namely the Old Law and the New Law.

I answer that, As stated in the First Part, distinction is the cause of number. Now things may be distinguished in two ways. First, as those things that are altogether specifically different, e.g. a horse and an ox. Secondly, as perfect and imperfect in the same species, e.g. a boy and a man: and in this way the Divine law is divided into Old and New. Hence the Apostle (Galatians 3:24, 25) compares the state of man under the Old Law to that of a child "under a pedagogue"; but the state under the New Law, to that of a full grown man, who is "no longer under a pedagogue."

Now the perfection and imperfection of these two laws is to be taken in connection with the three conditions pertaining to law, as stated above. For, in the first place, it belongs to law to be directed to the common good as to its end, as stated above. This good may be twofold. It may be a sensible and earthly good; and to this, man was directly ordained by the Old Law: wherefore, at the very outset of the law, the people were invited to the earthly kingdom of the Chananaeans (Exodus. 3:8, 17). Again it may be an intelligible and heavenly good: and to this, man is ordained by the New Law. Wherefore, at the very beginning of His preaching, Christ invited men to the kingdom of heaven, saying (Matthew. 4:17): "Do penance, for the kingdom of heaven is at hand." Hence Augustine says that "promises of temporal goods are contained in the Old Testament, for which reason it is called old; but the promise of eternal life belongs to the New Testament."

Secondly, it belongs to the law to direct human acts according to the order of righteousness: wherein also the New Law surpasses the Old Law, since it directs our internal acts, according to Matthew 5:20: "Unless your justice abound more than that of the Scribes and Pharisees, you shall not enter into the kingdom of heaven." Hence the saying that "the Old Law restrains the hand, but the New Law controls the mind."

Thirdly, it belongs to the law to induce men to observe its commandments. This the Old Law did by the fear of punishment: but the New Law, by love, which is poured into our hearts by the grace of Christ, bestowed in the New Law, but foreshadowed in the Old. Hence Augustine says that "there is little difference between the Law and the Gospel—fear and love."

Reply To Objection 1: As the father of a family issues different commands to the children and to the adults, so also the one King, God, in His one kingdom, gave one law to men, while they were yet imperfect, and another more perfect law, when, by the preceding law, they had been led to a greater capacity for Divine things.

Reply To Objection 2: The salvation of man could not be achieved otherwise than through Christ, according to Acts 4:12: "There is no other name . . . given to men, whereby we must be saved." Consequently the law that brings all to salvation could not be given until after the coming of Christ. But before His coming it was necessary to give to the people, of whom Christ was to be born, a law containing certain rudiments of righteousness unto salvation, in order to prepare them to receive Him.

Reply To Objection 3: The natural law directs man by way of certain general precepts, common to both the perfect and the imperfect: wherefore it is one and the same for all. But the Divine law directs man also in certain particular matters, to which the perfect and imperfect do not stand in the same relation. Hence the necessity for the Divine law to be twofold, as already explained.

FOUR

Thomas Hobbes

Thomas Hobbes (1588 - 1679) was born in the small English village of Westport. He was the son of a Catholic vicar but came under the care of his uncle, a merchant, when his father was forced to abandon his wife and children. Little else is known about Hobbes's upbringing.

Hobbes's most famous work, Leviathan, *was written later in life between the ages of 54 and 63 (he lived to be 91) under the shadow of the English Civil War (roughly 1642 - 1651). In the selection that follows, Hobbes postulates a hypothetical time in the history of humankind that predates law and civil society, a condition he refers to as the "state of nature." Hobbes uses this hypothetical state of nature as the backdrop to his explorations of human capacities, human differences, what he believes to be innate human drives, and the rights shared by all people in light of these factors.*

For Hobbes, one's rights are derivative of one's natural capacities and, as such, they differ from individual to individual. By virtue of the strong man's strength, for example, the strong man has the right to exercise his great strength, whereas a weaker man does not share this right given his inferiority with respect to strength. The weaker man, however, may be superior to the strong man with respect to his intellectual capacities and will therefore enjoy greater rights with respect to intellect. In the end, says Hobbes, these capacities balance out, making all humans roughly equal to one another.

A number of things follow from Hobbes's analysis of humans in the state of nature, some pertaining to ethics, and some pertaining to the political structures necessary for the maintenance of a civilized society. With respect to ethics, the excerpts that follow articulate the key tenets of "ethical egoism." With respect to politics, Hobbes's Leviathan *offers one of the earliest defenses of "social contractarianism."*

Hobbes's Leviathan
Life in the State of Nature

NATURE hath made men so equal in the faculties of body and mind as that, though there be found one man sometimes manifestly stronger in body or of quicker mind than another, yet when all is reckoned together the difference between man and man is not so considerable as that one man can thereupon claim to himself any benefit to which another may not pretend as well as he. For as to the strength of body, the weakest has strength enough to kill the strongest, either by secret machination or by confederacy with others that are in the same danger with himself.

And as to the faculties of the mind, setting aside the arts grounded upon words, and especially that skill of proceeding upon general and infallible rules, called science, which very few have and but in few things, as being not a native faculty born with us, nor attained, as prudence, while we look after somewhat else, I find yet a greater equality amongst men than that of strength. For prudence is but experience, which equal time equally bestows on all men in those things they equally apply themselves unto. That which may perhaps make such equality incredible is but a vain conceit of one's own wisdom, which almost all men think they have in a greater degree than the vulgar; that is, than all men but themselves, and a few others, whom by fame, or for concurring with themselves, they approve. For such is the nature of men that howsoever they may acknowledge many others to be more witty, or more eloquent or more learned, yet they will hardly believe there be many so wise as themselves; for they see their own wit at hand, and other men's at a distance. But this proveth rather that men are in that point equal, than unequal. For there is not ordinarily a greater sign of the equal distribution of anything than that every man is contented with his share.

From this equality of ability ariseth equality of hope in the attaining of our ends. And therefore if any two men desire the same thing, which nevertheless they cannot both enjoy, they become enemies; and in the way to their end (which is principally their own conservation, and sometimes their delectation only) endeavour to destroy or subdue one another. And from hence it comes to pass that where an invader hath no more to fear than another man's single power, if one plant, sow, build, or possess a convenient seat, others may probably be expected to come prepared with forces united to dispossess and deprive him, not only of the fruit of his labour, but also of his life or liberty. And the invader again is in the like danger of another.

And from this diffidence of one another, there is no way for any man to secure himself so reasonable as anticipation; that is, by force, or wiles, to master the persons of all men he can so long till he see no other power great enough to endanger him: and this is no more than his own conservation requireth, and is generally allowed. Also, because there be some that, taking pleasure in contemplating their own power in the acts of conquest, which they pursue farther than their security requires, if others, that otherwise would be glad to be at ease within modest bounds, should not by invasion increase their power, they would not be able, long time, by standing only on their defence, to subsist. And by consequence, such augmentation of dominion over men being necessary to a man's conservation, it ought to be allowed him.

Again, men have no pleasure (but on the contrary a great deal of grief) in keeping company where there is no power able to overawe them all. For every man looketh that his companion should value him at the same rate he sets upon himself, and upon all signs of contempt or undervaluing naturally endeavours, as far as he dares (which amongst them that have no common power to keep them in quiet is far enough to make them destroy each other), to extort a greater value from his contemners, by damage; and from others, by the example.

So that in the nature of man, we find three principal causes of quarrel. First, competition; secondly, diffidence; thirdly, glory.

The first maketh men invade for gain; the second, for safety; and the third, for reputation. The first use violence, to make themselves masters of other men's persons, wives, children, and cattle; the second, to defend them; the third, for trifles, as a word, a smile, a different opinion, and any other sign of undervalue, either direct in their persons or by reflection in their kindred, their friends, their nation, their profession, or their name.

Hereby it is manifest that during the time men live without a common power to keep them all in awe, they are in that condition which is called war; and such a war as is of every man against every man. For war consisteth not in battle only, or the act of fighting, but in a tract of time, wherein the will to contend by battle is sufficiently known: and therefore the notion of time is to be considered in the nature of war, as it is in the nature of weather. For as the nature of foul weather lieth not in a shower or two of rain, but in an inclination thereto of many days together: so the nature of war consisteth not in actual fighting, but in the known disposition thereto during all the time there is no assurance to the contrary. All other time is peace.

Whatsoever therefore is consequent to a time of war, where every man is enemy to every man, the same consequent to the time wherein men live without other security than what their own strength and their own invention shall furnish them withal. In such condition there is no place for industry, because the fruit thereof is uncertain: and consequently no culture of the earth; no navigation, nor use of the commodities that may be imported by sea; no commodious building; no instruments of moving and removing such things as require much force; no knowledge of the face of the earth; no account of time; no arts; no letters; no society; and which is worst of all, continual fear, and danger of violent death; and the life of man, solitary, poor, nasty, brutish, and short.

It may seem strange to some man that has not well weighed these things that Nature should thus dissociate and render men apt to invade and destroy one another: and he may therefore, not trusting to this inference, made from the passions, desire perhaps to have the same confirmed by experience. Let him therefore consider with himself: when taking a journey, he arms himself and seeks to go well accompanied; when going to sleep, he locks his doors; when even in his house he locks his chests; and this when he knows there be laws and public officers, armed, to revenge all injuries shall be done him; what opinion he has of his fellow subjects, when he rides armed; of his fellow citizens, when he locks his doors; and of his children, and servants, when he locks his chests. Does he not there as much accuse mankind by his actions as I do by my words? But neither of us accuse man's nature in it. The desires, and other passions of man, are in themselves no sin. No more are the actions that proceed from those passions till they know a law that forbids them; which till laws be made they cannot know, nor can any law be made till they have agreed upon the person that shall make it.

It may peradventure be thought there was never such a time nor condition of war as this; and I believe it was never generally so, over all the world: but there are many places where they live so now. For the savage people in many places of America, except the government of small families, the concord whereof dependeth on natural lust, have no government at all, and live at this day in that brutish manner, as I said before. Howsoever, it may be perceived what manner of life there would be, where there were no common power to fear, by the manner of life which men that have formerly lived under a peaceful government use to degenerate into a civil war.

But though there had never been any time wherein particular men were in a condition of war one against another, yet in all times kings and persons of sovereign authority, because of their independency, are in continual jealousies, and in the state and posture of gladiators, having their weapons pointing, and their eyes fixed on one another; that is, their forts, garrisons, and guns upon the frontiers of their kingdoms, and continual spies upon their neighbours, which is a posture of war. But because they uphold thereby the industry of their subjects, there does not follow from it that misery which accompanies the liberty of particular men.

To this war of every man against every man, this also is consequent; that nothing can be unjust. The notions of right and wrong, justice and injustice, have there no place. Where there is no common power, there is no law; where no law, no injustice. Force and fraud are in war the two cardinal virtues. Justice and injustice are none of the faculties neither of the body nor mind. If they were, they might be in a man that were alone in the world, as well as his senses and passions. They are qualities that relate to men in society, not in solitude. It is consequent also to the same condition that there be no propriety, no dominion, no mine and thine distinct; but only that to be every man's that he can get, and for so long as he can keep it. And thus much for the ill condition which man by mere nature is actually placed in; though with a possibility to come out of it, consisting partly in the passions, partly in his reason.

The passions that incline men to peace are: fear of death; desire of such things as are necessary to commodious living; and a hope by their industry to obtain them. And reason suggesteth convenient articles of peace upon which men may be drawn to agreement. These articles are they which otherwise are called the laws of nature, whereof I shall speak more particularly in the two following chapters.

Hobbes's Leviathan
The Laws of Nature

THE right of nature, which writers commonly call jus naturale, is the liberty each man hath to use his own power as he will himself for the preservation of his own nature; that is to say, of his own life; and consequently, of doing anything which, in his own judgement and reason, he shall conceive to be the aptest means thereunto.

By liberty is understood, according to the proper signification of the word, the absence of external impediments; which impediments may oft take away part of a man's power to do what he would, but cannot hinder him from using the power left him according as his judgement and reason shall dictate to him.

A law of nature, lex naturalis, is a precept, or general rule, found out by reason, by which a man is forbidden to do that which is destructive of his life, or taketh away the means of preserving the same, and to omit that by which he thinketh it may be best preserved. For though they that speak of this subject use to confound jus and lex, right and law, yet they ought to be distinguished, because right consisteth in liberty to do, or to forbear; whereas law determineth and bindeth to one of them: so that law and right differ as much as obligation and liberty, which in one and the same matter are inconsistent.

And because the condition of man (as hath been declared in the precedent chapter) is a condition of war of every one against every one, in which case every one is governed by his own reason, and there is nothing he can make use of that may not be a help unto him in preserving his life against his enemies; it followeth that in such a condition every man has a right to every thing, even to one another's body. And therefore, as long as this natural right of every man to every thing endureth, there can be no security to any man, how strong or wise soever he be, of living out the time which nature ordinarily alloweth men to live. And consequently it is a precept, or general rule of reason: that every man ought to endeavour peace, as far as he has hope of obtaining it; and when he cannot obtain it, that he may seek and use all helps and advantages of war. The first branch of which rule containeth the first and fundamental law of nature, which is: to seek peace and follow it. The second, the sum of the right of nature, which is: by all means we can to defend ourselves.

From this fundamental law of nature, by which men are commanded to endeavour peace, is derived this second law: that a man be willing, when others are so too, as far forth as for peace and defence of himself he shall think it necessary, to lay down this right to all things; and be contented with so much liberty against other men as he would allow other men against himself. For as long as every man holdeth this right, of doing anything he liketh; so long are all men in the condition of war. But if other men will not lay down their right, as well as he, then there is no reason for anyone to divest himself of his: for that were to expose himself to prey, which no man is bound to, rather than to dispose himself to peace. This is that law of the gospel: Whatsoever you require that others should do to you, that do ye to them. And that law of all men, quod tibi fieri non vis, alteri ne feceris.

To lay down a man's right to anything is to divest himself of the liberty of hindering another of the benefit of his own right to the same. For he that renounceth or passeth away his right giveth not to any other man a right which he had not before, because there is nothing to which every man had not right by nature, but only standeth out of his way that he may enjoy his own original right without hindrance from him, not without hindrance from another. So that the effect which redoundeth to one man by another man's defect of right is but so much diminution of impediments to the use of his own right original.

Right is laid aside, either by simply renouncing it, or by transferring it to another. By simply renouncing, when he cares not to whom the benefit thereof redoundeth. By transferring, when he intendeth the benefit thereof to some certain person or persons. And when a man hath in either manner abandoned or granted away his right, then is he said to be obliged, or bound, not to hinder those to whom such right is granted, or abandoned, from the benefit of it: and that he ought, and it is duty, not to make void that voluntary act of his own: and that such hindrance is injustice, and injury, as being sine jure; the right being before renounced or transferred. So that injury or injustice, in the controversies of the world, is somewhat like to that which in the disputations of scholars is called absurdity. For as it is there called an absurdity to contradict what one maintained in the beginning; so in the world it is called injustice, and injury voluntarily to undo that which from the beginning he had voluntarily done. The way by which a man either simply renounceth or transferreth his right is a declaration, or signification, by some voluntary and sufficient sign, or signs, that he doth so renounce or transfer, or hath so renounced or transferred the same, to him that accepteth it. And these signs are either words only, or actions only; or, as it happeneth most often, both words and actions. And the same are the bonds, by which men are bound and obliged: bonds that have their strength, not from their own nature (for nothing is more easily broken than a man's word), but from fear of some evil consequence upon the rupture.

Whensoever a man transferreth his right, or renounceth it, it is either in consideration of some right reciprocally transferred to himself, or for some other good he hopeth for thereby. For it is a voluntary act: and of the voluntary acts of every man, the object is some good to himself. And therefore there be some rights which no man can be understood by any words, or other signs, to have abandoned or transferred. As first a man cannot lay down the right of resisting them that assault him by force to take away his life, because he cannot be understood to aim thereby at any good to himself. The same may be said of wounds, and chains, and imprisonment, both because there is no benefit consequent to such patience, as there is to the patience of suffering another to be wounded or imprisoned, as also because a man cannot tell when he seeth men proceed against him by violence whether they intend his death or not. And lastly the motive and end for which this renouncing and transferring of right is introduced is nothing else but the security of a man's person, in his life, and in the means of so preserving life as not to be weary of it. And therefore if a man by words, or other signs, seem to despoil himself of the end for which those signs were intended, he is not to be understood as if he meant it, or that it was his will, but that he was ignorant of how such words and actions were to be interpreted.

The mutual transferring of right is that which men call contract.

There is difference between transferring of right to the thing, the thing, and transferring or tradition, that is, delivery of the thing itself. For the thing may be delivered together with the translation of the right, as in buying and selling with ready money, or exchange of goods or lands, and it may be delivered some time after.

Again, one of the contractors may deliver the thing contracted for on his part, and leave the other to perform his part at some determinate time after, and in the meantime be trusted; and then the contract on his part is called pact, or covenant: or both parts may contract now to perform hereafter, in which cases he that is to perform in time to come, being trusted, his performance is called keeping of promise, or faith, and the failing of performance, if it be voluntary, violation of faith.

When the transferring of right is not mutual, but one of the parties transferreth in hope to gain thereby friendship or service from another, or from his friends; or in hope to gain the reputation of charity, or magnanimity; or to deliver his mind from the pain of compassion; or in hope of reward in heaven; this is not contract, but gift, free gift, grace: which words signify one and the same thing.

Signs of contract are either express or by inference. Express are words spoken with understanding of what they signify: and such words are either of the time present or past; as, I give, I grant, I have given, I have granted, I will that this be yours: or of the future; as, I will give, I will grant, which words of the future are called promise.

Signs by inference are sometimes the consequence of words; sometimes the consequence of silence; sometimes the consequence of actions; sometimes the consequence of forbearing an action: and generally a sign by inference, of any contract, is whatsoever sufficiently argues the will of the contractor.

Words alone, if they be of the time to come, and contain a bare promise, are an insufficient sign of a free gift and therefore not obligatory. For if they be of the time to come, as, tomorrow I will give, they are a sign I have not given yet, and consequently that my right is not transferred, but remaineth till I transfer it by some other act. But if the words be of the time present, or past, as, I have given, or do give to be delivered tomorrow, then is my tomorrow's right given away today; and that by the virtue of the words, though there were no other argument of my will. And there is a great difference in the signification of these words, volo hoc tuum esse cras, and cras dabo; that is, between I will that this be thine tomorrow, and, I will give it thee tomorrow: for the word I will, in the former manner of speech, signifies an act of the will present; but in the latter, it signifies a promise of an act of the will to come: and therefore the former words, being of the present, transfer a future right; the latter, that be of the future, transfer nothing. But if there be other signs of the will to transfer a right besides words; then, though the gift be free, yet may the right be understood to pass by words of the future: as if a man propound a prize to him that comes first to the end of a race, the gift is free; and though the words be of the future, yet the right passeth: for if he would not have his words so be understood, he should not have let them run.

In contracts the right passeth, not only where the words are of the time present or past, but also where they are of the future, because all contract is mutual translation, or change of right; and therefore he that promiseth only, because he hath already received the benefit for which he promiseth, is to be understood as if he intended the right should pass: for unless he had been content to have his words so understood, the other would not have performed his part first. And for that cause, in buying, and selling, and other acts of contract, a promise is equivalent to a covenant, and therefore obligatory.

He that performeth first in the case of a contract is said to merit that which he is to receive by the performance of the other, and he hath it as due. Also when a prize is propounded to many, which is to be given to him only that winneth,or money is thrown amongst many to be enjoyed by them that catch it; though this be a free gift, yet so to win, or so to catch, is to merit, and to have it as due. For the right is transferred in the propounding of the prize, and in throwing down the money, though it be not determined to whom, but by the event of the contention. But there is between these two sorts of merit this difference, that in contract I merit by virtue of my own power and the contractor's need, but in this case of free gift I am enabled to merit only by the benignity of the giver: in contract I merit at the contractor's hand that he should depart with his right; in this case of gift, I merit not that the giver should part with his right, but that when he has parted with it, it should be mine rather than another's. And this I think to be the meaning of that distinction of the Schools between meritum congrui and meritum condigni. For God Almighty, having promised paradise to those men, hoodwinked with carnal desires, that can walk through this world according to the precepts and limits prescribed by him, they say he that shall so walk shall merit paradise ex congruo. But because no man can demand a right to it by his own righteousness, or any other power in himself, but by the free grace of God only, they say no man can merit paradise ex condigno. This, I say, I think is the meaning of that distinction; but because disputers do not agree upon the signification of their own terms of art longer than it serves their turn, I will not affirm anything of their meaning: only this I say; when a gift is given indefinitely, as a prize to be contended for, he that winneth meriteth, and may claim the prize as due.

If a covenant be made wherein neither of the parties perform presently, but trust one another, in the condition of mere nature (which is a condition of war of every man against every man) upon any reasonable suspicion, it is void: but if there be a common power set over them both, with right and force sufficient to compel performance, it is not void. For he that performeth first has no assurance the other will perform after, because the bonds of words are too weak to bridle men's ambition, avarice, anger, and other passions, without the fear of some coercive power; which in the condition of mere nature, where all men are equal, and judges of the justness of their own fears, cannot possibly be supposed. And therefore he which performeth first does but betray himself to his enemy, contrary to the right he can never abandon of defending his life and means of living.

But in a civil estate, where there a power set up to constrain those that would otherwise violate their faith, that fear is no more reasonable; and for that cause, he which by the covenant is to perform first is obliged so to do.

The cause of fear, which maketh such a covenant invalid, must be always something arising after the covenant made, as some new fact or other sign of the will not to perform, else it cannot make the covenant void. For that which could not hinder a man from promising ought not to be admitted as a hindrance of performing.

He that transferreth any right transferreth the means of enjoying it, as far as lieth in his power. As he that selleth land is understood to transfer the herbage and whatsoever grows upon it; nor can he that sells a mill turn away the stream that drives it. And they that give to a man the right of government in sovereignty are understood to give him the right of levying money to maintain soldiers, and of appointing magistrates for the administration of justice.

To make covenants with brute beasts is impossible, because not understanding our speech, they understand not, nor accept of any translation of right, nor can translate any right to another: and without mutual acceptation, there is no covenant.

To make covenant with God is impossible but by mediation of such as God speaketh to, either by revelation supernatural or by His lieutenants that govern under Him and in His name: for otherwise we know not whether our covenants be accepted or not. And therefore they that vow anything contrary to any law of nature, vow in vain, as being a thing unjust to pay such vow. And if it be a thing commanded by the law of nature, it is not the vow, but the law that binds them.

The matter or subject of a covenant is always something that falleth under deliberation, for to covenant is an act of the will; that is to say, an act, and the last act, of deliberation; and is therefore always understood to be something to come, and which judged possible for him that covenanteth to perform.

And therefore, to promise that which is known to be impossible is no covenant. But if that prove impossible afterwards, which before was thought possible, the covenant is valid and bindeth, though not to the thing itself, yet to the value; or, if that also be impossible, to the unfeigned endeavour of performing as much as is possible, for to more no man can be obliged.

Men are freed of their covenants two ways; by performing, or by being forgiven. For performance is the natural end of obligation, and forgiveness the restitution of liberty, as being a retransferring of that right in which the obligation consisted.

Covenants entered into by fear, in the condition of mere nature, are obligatory. For example, if I covenant to pay a ransom, or service for my life, to an enemy, I am bound by it. For it is a contract, wherein one receiveth the benefit of life; the other is to receive money, or service for it, and consequently, where no other law (as in the condition of mere nature) forbiddeth the performance, the covenant is valid. Therefore prisoners of war, if trusted with the payment of their ransom, are obliged to pay it: and if a weaker prince make a disadvantageous peace with a stronger, for fear, he is bound to keep it; unless (as hath been said before) there ariseth some new and just cause of fear to renew the war. And even in Commonwealths, if I be forced to redeem myself from a thief by promising him money, I am bound to pay it, till the civil law discharge me. For whatsoever I may lawfully do without obligation, the same I may lawfully covenant to do through fear: and what I lawfully covenant, I cannot lawfully break.

A former covenant makes void a later. For a man that hath passed away his right to one man today hath it not to pass tomorrow to another: and therefore the later promise passeth no right, but is null.

A covenant not to defend myself from force, by force, is always void. For (as I have shown before) no man can transfer or lay down his right to save himself from death, wounds, and imprisonment, the avoiding whereof is the only end of laying down any right; and therefore the promise of not resisting force, in no covenant transferreth any right, nor is obliging. For though a man may covenant thus, unless I do so, or so, kill me; he cannot covenant thus, unless I do so, or so, I will not resist you when you come to kill me. For man by nature chooseth the lesser evil, which is danger of death in resisting, rather than the greater, which is certain and present death in not resisting. And this is granted to be true by all men, in that they lead criminals to execution, and prison, with armed men, notwithstanding that such criminals have consented to the law by which they are condemned.

A covenant to accuse oneself, without assurance of pardon, is likewise invalid. For in the condition of nature where every man is judge, there is no place for accusation: and in the civil state the accusation is followed with punishment, which, being force, a man is not obliged not to resist. The same is also true of the accusation of those by whose condemnation a man falls into misery; as of a father, wife, or benefactor. For the testimony of such an accuser, if it be not willingly given, is presumed to be corrupted by nature, and therefore not to be received: and where a man's testimony is not to be credited, he is not bound to give it. Also accusations upon torture are not to be reputed as testimonies. For torture is to be used but as means of conjecture, and light, in the further examination and search of truth: and what is in that case confessed tendeth to the ease of him that is tortured, not to the informing of the torturers, and therefore ought not to have the credit of a sufficient testimony: for whether he deliver himself by true or false accusation, he does it by the right of preserving his own life.

The force of words being (as I have formerly noted) too weak to hold men to the performance of their covenants, there are in man's nature but two imaginable helps to strengthen it. And those are either a fear of the consequence of breaking their word, or a glory or pride in appearing not to need to break it. This latter is a generosity too rarely found to be presumed on, especially in the pursuers of wealth, command, or sensual pleasure, which are the greatest part of mankind. The passion to be reckoned upon is fear; whereof there be two very general objects: one, the power of spirits invisible; the other, the power of those men they shall therein offend. Of these two, though the former be the greater power, yet the fear of the latter is commonly the greater fear. The fear of the former is in every man his own religion, which hath place in the nature of man before civil society. The latter hath not so; at least not place enough to keep men to their promises, because in the condition of mere nature, the inequality of power is not discerned, but by the event of battle. So that before the time of civil society, or in the interruption thereof by war, there is nothing can strengthen a covenant of peace agreed on against the temptations of avarice, ambition, lust, or other strong desire, but the fear of that invisible power which they every one worship as God, and fear as a revenger of their perfidy. All therefore that can be done between two men not subject to civil power is to put one another to swear by the God he feareth: which swearing, or oath, is a form of speech, added to a promise, by which he that promiseth signifieth that unless he perform he renounceth the mercy of his God, or calleth to him for vengeance on himself. Such was the heathen form, Let Jupiter kill me else, as I kill this beast. So is our form, I shall do thus, and thus, so help me God. And this, with the rites and ceremonies which every one useth in his own religion, that the fear of breaking faith might be the greater.

By this it appears that an oath taken according to any other form, or rite, than his that sweareth is in vain and no oath, and that there is no swearing by anything which the swearer thinks not God. For though men have sometimes used to swear by their kings, for fear, or flattery; yet they would have it thereby understood they attributed to them divine honour. And that swearing unnecessarily by God is but profaning of his name: and swearing by other things, as men do in common discourse, is not swearing, but an impious custom, gotten by too much vehemence of talking.

It appears also that the oath adds nothing to the obligation. For a covenant, if lawful, binds in the sight of God, without the oath, as much as with it; if unlawful, bindeth not at all, though it be confirmed with an oath.

FIVE

John Locke

John Locke (1632 - 1704) was born just outside of Bristol, England. His father, a lawyer was also a cavalryman who fought for the Parliament during the English Civil War. Locke enjoyed considerable privilege throughout his upbringing, having been educated in some of the most prestigious schools of his day before studying medicine at Oxford University. Locke's first career was as a physician. As the personal physician to the First Earl of Shaftesbury, Locke became interested in politics and eventually became heavily involved in the Whig movement, a political movement founded by his patron, the First Earl of Shaftesbury.

Locke's writing spans a wide variety of topics, including politics and government, law and legislation, psychology, epistemology, education, and religious tolerance. Locke is considered the father of modern liberalism and his work has made a direct impact upon the constitutions of most of the World's democratic states.

The selections included are drawn from Locke's Second Treatise on Government. *In the first excerpt we find Locke's reprisal of the notion employed by Hobbes to explore the human condition--specifically, the state of nature. Locke's is a kinder, gentler state of nature, in which humanity shares a natural inclination towards cooperation. This has subtle but significant implications for the precepts of law, government, and ethics in general.*

The second excerpt is Locke's highly influential discussion of property and what entitles an individual to claim right of property over something. This text is particularly relevant to, and has been particularly influential in, recent scholarly discussions concerning intellectual property rights.

Locke's Second Treatise
A Kinder State of Nature

4 TO understand political power right, and derive it from its original, we must consider, what state all men are naturally in, and that is, a state of perfect freedom to order their actions, and dispose of their possessions and persons, as they think fit, within the bounds of the law of nature, without asking leave, or depending upon the will of any other man.

A state also of equality, wherein all the power and jurisdiction is reciprocal, no one having more than another; there being nothing more evident, than that creatures of the same species and rank, promiscuously born to all the same advantages of nature, and the use of the same faculties, should also be equal one amongst another without subordination or subjection, unless the lord and master of them all should, by any manifest declaration of his will, set one above another, and confer on him, by an evident and clear appointment, an undoubted right to dominion and sovereignty.

5 This equality of men by nature, the judicious Hooker looks upon as so evident in itself, and beyond all question, that he makes it the foundation of that obligation to mutual love amongst men, on which he builds the duties they owe one another, and from whence he derives the great maxims of justice and charity. His words are,

The like natural inducement hath brought men to know that it is no less their duty, to love others than themselves; for seeing those things which are equal, must needs all have one measure; if I cannot but wish to receive good, even as much at every man's hands, as any man can wish unto his own soul, how should I look to have any part of my desire herein satisfied, unless myself be careful to satisfy the like desire, which is undoubtedly in other men, being of one and the same nature? To have any thing offered them repugnant to this desire, must needs in all respects grieve them as much as me; so that if I do harm, I must look to suffer, there being no reason that others should shew greater measure of love to me, than they have by me shewed unto them: my desire therefore to be loved of my equals in nature as much as possible may be, imposeth upon me a natural duty of bearing to them-ward fully the like affection; from which relation of equality between ourselves and them that are as ourselves, what several rules and canons natural reason hath drawn, for direction of life, no man is ignorant, Eccl. Pol. Lib. 1.

6 But though this be a state of liberty, yet it is not a state of licence: though man in that state have an uncontroulable liberty to dispose of his person or possessions, yet he has not liberty to destroy himself, or so much as any creature in his possession, but where some nobler use than its bare preservation calls for it. The state of nature has a law of nature to govern it, which obliges every one: and reason, which is that law, teaches all mankind, who will but consult it, that being all equal and independent, no one ought to harm another in his life, health, liberty, or possessions: for men being all the workmanship of one omnipotent, and infinitely wise maker; all the servants of one sovereign master, sent into the world by his order, and about his business; they are his property, whose workmanship they are, made to last during his, not one another's pleasure: and being furnished with like faculties, sharing all in one community of nature, there cannot be supposed any such subordination among us, that may authorize us to destroy one another, as if we were made for one another's uses, as the inferior ranks of creatures are for our's. Every one, as he is bound to preserve himself, and not to quit his station wilfully, so by the like reason, when his own preservation comes not in competition, ought he, as much as he can, to preserve the rest of mankind, and may not, unless it be to do justice on an offender, take away, or impair the life, or what tends to the preservation of the life, the liberty, health, limb, or goods of another.

7 And that all men may be restrained from invading others rights, and from doing hurt to one another, and the law of nature be observed, which willeth the peace and preservation of all mankind, the execution of the law of nature is, in that state, put into every man's hands, whereby every one has a right to punish the transgressors of that law to such a degree, as may hinder its violation: for the law of nature would, as all other laws that concern men in this world 'be in vain, if there were no body that in the state of nature had a power to execute that law, and thereby preserve the innocent and restrain offenders. And if any one in the state of nature may punish another for any evil he has done, every one may do so: for in that state of perfect equality, where naturally there is no superiority or jurisdiction of one over another, what any may do in prosecution of that law, every one must needs have a right to do.

8 And thus, in the state of nature, one man comes by a power over another; but yet no absolute or arbitrary power, to use a criminal, when he has got him in his hands, according to the passionate heats, or boundless extravagancy of his own will; but only to retribute to him, so far as calm reason and conscience dictate, what is proportionate to his transgression, which is so much as may serve for reparation and restraint: for these two are the only reasons, why one man may lawfully do harm to another, which is that we call punishment. In transgressing the law of nature, the offender declares himself to live by another rule than that of reason and common equity, which is that measure God has set to the actions of men, for their mutual security; and so he becomes dangerous to mankind, the tye, which is to secure them from injury and violence, being slighted and broken by him. Which being a trespass against the whole species, and the peace and safety of it, provided for by the law of nature, every man upon this score, by the right he hath to preserve mankind in general, may restrain, or where it is necessary, destroy things noxious to them, and so may bring such evil on any one, who hath transgressed that law, as may make him repent the doing of it, and thereby deter him, and by his example others, from doing the like mischief. And in the case, and upon this ground, EVERY MAN HATH A RIGHT TO PUNISH THE OFFENDER, AND BE EXECUTIONER OF THE LAW OF NATURE.

9 I doubt not but this will seem a very strange doctrine to some men: but before they condemn it, I desire them to resolve me, by what right any prince or state can put to death, or punish an alien, for any crime he commits in their country. It is certain their laws, by virtue of any sanction they receive from the promulgated will of the legislative, reach not a stranger: they speak not to him, nor, if they did, is he bound to hearken to them. The legislative authority, by which they are in force over the subjects of that commonwealth, hath no power over him. Those who have the supreme power of making laws in England, France or Holland, are to an Indian, but like the rest of the world, men without authority: and therefore, if by the law of nature every man hath not a power to punish offences against it, as he soberly judges the case to require, I see not how the magistrates of any community can punish an alien of another country; since, in reference to him, they can have no more power than what every man naturally may have over another.

10 Besides the crime which consists in violating the law, and varying from the right rule of reason, whereby a man so far becomes degenerate, and declares himself to quit the principles of

human nature, and to be a noxious creature, there is commonly injury done to some person or other, and some other man receives damage by his transgression: in which case he who hath received any damage, has, besides the right of punishment common to him with other men, a particular right to seek reparation from him that has done it: and any other person, who finds it just, may also join with him that is injured, and assist him in recovering from the offender so much as may make satisfaction for the harm he has suffered.

11 From these two distinct rights, the one of punishing the crime for restraint, and preventing the like offence, which right of punishing is in every body; the other of taking reparation, which belongs only to the injured party, comes it to pass that the magistrate, who by being magistrate hath the common right of punishing put into his hands, can often, where the public good demands not the execution of the law, remit the punishment of criminal offences by his own authority, but yet cannot remit the satisfaction due to any private man for the damage he has received. That, he who has suffered the damage has a right to demand in his own name, and he alone can remit: the damnified person has this power of appropriating to himself the goods or service of the offender, by right of self-preservation, as every man has a power to punish the crime, to prevent its being committed again, by the right he has of preserving all mankind, and doing all reasonable things he can in order to that end: and thus it is, that every man, in the state of nature, has a power to kill a murderer, both to deter others from doing the like injury, which no reparation can compensate, by the example of the punishment that attends it from every body, and also to secure men from the attempts of a criminal, who having renounced reason, the common rule and measure God hath given to mankind, hath, by the unjust violence and slaughter he hath committed upon one, declared war against all mankind, and therefore may be destroyed as a lion or a tyger, one of those wild savage beasts, with whom men can have no society nor security: and upon this is grounded that great law of nature, Whoso sheddeth man's blood, by man shall his blood be shed. And Cain was so fully convinced, that every one had a right to destroy such a criminal, that after the murder of his brother, he cries out, Every one that findeth me, shall slay me; so plain was it writ in the hearts of all mankind.

12 By the same reason may a man in the state of nature punish the lesser breaches of that law. It will perhaps be demanded, with death? I answer, each transgression may be punished to that degree, and with so much severity, as will suffice to make it an ill

bargain to the offender, give him cause to repent, and terrify others from doing the like. Every offence, that can be committed in the state of nature, may in the state of nature be also punished equally, and as far forth as it may, in a commonwealth: for though it would be besides my present purpose, to enter here into the particulars of the law of nature, or its measures of punishment; yet, it is certain there is such a law, and that too, as intelligible and plain to a rational creature, and a studier of that law, as the positive laws of commonwealths; nay, possibly plainer; as much as reason is easier to be understood, than the fancies and intricate contrivances of men, following contrary and hidden interests put into words; for so truly are a great part of the municipal laws of countries, which are only so far right, as they are founded on the law of nature, by which they are to be regulated and interpreted.

13 To this strange doctrine, viz. That in the state of nature every one has the executive power of the law of nature, I doubt not but it will be objected, that it is unreasonable for men to be judges in their own cases, that self-love will make men partial to themselves and their friends: and on the other side, that ill nature, passion and revenge will carry them too far in punishing others; and hence nothing but confusion and disorder will follow, and that therefore God hath certainly appointed government to restrain the partiality and violence of men. I easily grant, that civil government is the proper remedy for the inconveniencies of the state of nature, which must certainly be great, where men may be judges in their own case, since it is easy to be imagined, that he who was so unjust as to do his brother an injury, will scarce be so just as to condemn himself for it: but I shall desire those who make this objection, to remember, that absolute monarchs are but men; and if government is to be the remedy of those evils, which necessarily follow from men's being judges in their own cases, and the state of nature is therefore not to be endured, I desire to know what kind of government that is, and how much better it is than the state of nature, where one man, commanding a multitude, has the liberty to be judge in his own case, and may do to all his subjects whatever he pleases, without the least liberty to any one to question or controul those who execute his pleasure? and in whatsoever he doth, whether led by reason, mistake or passion, must be submitted to? much better it is in the state of nature, wherein men are not bound to submit to the unjust will of another: and if he that judges, judges amiss in his own, or any other case, he is answerable for it to the rest of mankind.

14 It is often asked as a mighty objection, where are, or ever were there any men in such a state of nature? To which it may suffice as an answer at present, that since all princes and rulers of independent governments all through the world, are in a state of nature, it is plain the world never was, nor ever will be, without numbers of men in that state. I have named all governors of independent communities, whether they are, or are not, in league with others: for it is not every compact that puts an end to the state of nature between men, but only this one of agreeing together mutually to enter into one community, and make one body politic; other promises, and compacts, men may make one with another, and yet still be in the state of nature. The promises and bargains for truck, &c. between the two men in the desert island, mentioned by Garcilasso de la Vega, in his history of Peru; or between a Swiss and an Indian, in the woods of America, are binding to them, though they are perfectly in a state of nature, in reference to one another: for truth and keeping of faith belongs to men, as men, and not as members of society.

15 To those that say, there were never any men in the state of nature, I will not only oppose the authority of the judicious Hooker, Eccl. Pol. lib. i. sect. 10, where he says,

The laws which have been hitherto mentioned, i.e. the laws of nature, do bind men absolutely, even as they are men, although they have never any settled fellowship, never any solemn agreement amongst themselves what to do, or not to do: but forasmuch as we are not by ourselves sufficient to furnish ourselves with competent store of things, needful for such a life as our nature doth desire, a life fit for the dignity of man; therefore to supply those defects and imperfections which are in us, as living single and solely by ourselves, we are naturally induced to seek communion and fellowship with others: this was the cause of men's uniting themselves at first in politic societies.

But I moreover affirm, that all men are naturally in that state, and remain so, till by their own consents they make themselves members of some politic society; and I doubt not in the sequel of this discourse, to make it very clear.

Locke's Second Treatise
Of Property

26 God, who hath given the world to men in common, hath also given them reason to make use of it to the best advantage of life, and convenience. The earth, and all that is therein, is given to men for the support and comfort of their being. And tho' all the fruits it naturally produces, and beasts it feeds, belong to mankind in common, as they are produced by the spontaneous hand of nature; and no body has originally a private dominion, exclusive of the rest of mankind, in any of them, as they are thus in their natural state: yet being given for the use of men, there must of necessity be a means to appropriate them some way or other, before they can be of any use, or at all beneficial to any particular man. The fruit, or venison, which nourishes the wild Indian, who knows no enclosure, and is still a tenant in common, must be his, and so his, i.e. a part of him, that another can no longer have any right to it, before it can do him any good for the support of his life.

27 Though the earth, and all inferior creatures, be common to all men, yet every man has a property in his own person: this no body has any right to but himself. The labour of his body, and the work of his hands, we may say, are properly his. Whatsoever then he removes out of the state that nature hath provided, and left it in, he hath mixed his labour with, and joined to it something that is his own, and thereby makes it his property. It being by him removed from the common state nature hath placed it in, it hath by this labour something annexed to it, that excludes the common right of other men: for this labour being the unquestionable property of the labourer, no man but he can have a right to what that is once joined to, at least where there is enough, and as good, left in common for others…

32 But the chief matter of property being now not the fruits of the earth, and the beasts that subsist on it, but the earth itself; as that which takes in and carries with it all the rest; I think it is plain, that property in that too is acquired as the former. As much land as a man tills, plants, improves, cultivates, and can use the product of, so much is his property. He by his labour does, as it were, inclose it from the common. Nor will it invalidate his right, to say every body else has an equal title to it; and therefore he cannot appropriate, he cannot inclose, without the consent of all his fellow-commoners, all mankind. God, when he gave the world in common to all mankind, commanded man also to labour, and the penury of his condition required it of him. God and his reason commanded him to subdue the earth, i.e. improve it for the benefit of life, and therein lay out something upon it that was his own, his labour. He that in obedience to this command of God, subdued, tilled and sowed any part of it, thereby annexed to it something that was his property, which another had no title to, nor could without injury take from him.

33 Nor was this appropriation of any parcel of land, by improving it, any prejudice to any other man, since there was still enough, and as good left; and more than the yet unprovided could use. So that, in effect, there was never the less left for others because of his enclosure for himself: for he that leaves as much as another can make use of, does as good as take nothing at all. No body could think himself injured by the drinking of another man, though he took a good draught, who had a whole river of the same water left him to quench his thirst: and the case of land and water, where there is enough of both, is perfectly the same.

34 God gave the world to men in common; but since he gave it them for their benefit, and the greatest conveniencies of life they were capable to draw from it, it cannot be supposed he meant it should always remain common and uncultivated. He gave it to the use of the industrious and rational, (and labour was to be his title to it;) not to the fancy or covetousness of the quarrelsome and contentious. He that had as good left for his improvement, as was already taken up, needed not complain, ought not to meddle with what was already improved by another's labour: if he did, it is plain he desired the benefit of another's pains, which he had no right to, and not the ground which God had given him in common with others to labour on, and whereof there was as good left, as that already possessed, and more than he knew what to do with, or his industry could reach to.

35 It is true, in land that is common in England, or any other country, where there is plenty of people under government, who have money and commerce, no one can inclose or appropriate any part, without the consent of all his fellow-commoners; because this is left common by compact, i.e. by the law of the land, which is not to be violated. And though it be common, in respect of some men, it is not so to all mankind; but is the joint property of this country, or this parish. Besides, the remainder, after such enclosure, would not be as good to the rest of the commoners, as the whole was when they could all make use of the whole; whereas in the beginning and first peopling of the great common of the world, it was quite otherwise. The law man was under, was rather for appropriating. God commanded, and his wants forced him to labour. That was his property which could not be taken from him where-ever he had fixed it. And hence subduing or cultivating the earth, and having dominion, we see are joined together. The one gave title to the other. So that God, by commanding to subdue, gave authority so far to appropriate: and the condition of human life, which requires labour and materials to work on, necessarily introduces private possessions.

36 The measure of property nature has well set by the extent of men's labour and the conveniencies of life: no man's labour could subdue, or appropriate all; nor could his enjoyment consume more than a small part; so that it was impossible for any man, this way, to intrench upon the right of another, or acquire to himself a property, to the prejudice of his neighbour, who would still have room for as good, and as large a possession (after the other had taken out his) as before it was appropriated. This measure did confine every man's possession to a very moderate proportion, and such as he might appropriate to himself, without injury to any body, in the first ages of the world, when men were more in danger to be lost, by wandering from their company, in the then vast wilderness of the earth, than to be straitened for want of room to plant in. And the same measure may be allowed still without prejudice to any body, as full as the world seems: for supposing a man, or family, in the state they were at first peopling of the world by the children of Adam, or Noah; let him plant in some inland, vacant places of America, we shall find that the possessions he could make himself, upon the measures we have given, would not be very large, nor, even to this day, prejudice the rest of mankind, or give them reason to complain, or think themselves injured by this man's incroachment, though the race of men have now spread themselves to all the corners of the world, and do infinitely exceed the small number was at the beginning. Nay, the extent of ground is of so little value, without labour, that I have heard it affirmed, that in Spain itself a man may be permitted to plough, sow and reap, without being disturbed, upon land he has no other title to, but only his making use of it. But, on the contrary, the inhabitants think themselves beholden to him, who, by his industry on neglected, and consequently waste land, has increased the stock of corn, which they wanted. But be this as it will, which I lay no stress on; this I dare boldly affirm, that the same rule of propriety, (viz.) that every man should have as much as he could make use of, would hold still in the world, without straitening any body; since there is land enough in the world to suffice double the inhabitants, had not the invention of money, and the tacit agreement of men to put a value on it, introduced (by consent) larger possessions, and a right to them; which, how it has done, I shall by and by shew more at large.

37 This is certain, that in the beginning, before the desire of having more than man needed had altered the intrinsic value of things, which depends only on their usefulness to the life of man; or had agreed, that a little piece of yellow metal, which would keep without wasting or decay, should be worth a great piece of flesh, or a whole heap of corn; though men had a right to appropriate, by their labour, each one of himself, as much of the things of nature, as he could use: yet this could not be much, nor to the prejudice of others, where the same plenty was still left to those who would use the same industry. To which let me add, that he who appropriates land to himself by his labour, does not lessen, but increase the common stock of mankind: for the provisions serving to the support of human life, produced by one acre of inclosed and cultivated land, are (to speak much within compass) ten times more than those which are yielded by an acre of land of an equal richness lying waste in common. And therefore he that incloses land, and has a greater plenty of the conveniencies of life from ten acres, than he could have from an hundred left to nature, may truly be said to give ninety acres to mankind: for his labour now supplies him with provisions out of ten acres, which were but the product of an hundred lying in common. I have here rated the improved land very low, in making its product but as ten to one, when it is much nearer an hundred to one: for I ask, whether in the wild woods and uncultivated waste of America, left to nature, without any improvement, tillage or husbandry, a thousand acres yield the needy and wretched inhabitants as many conveniencies of life, as ten acres of equally fertile land do in Devonshire, where they are well cultivated?

Before the appropriation of land, he who gathered as much of the wild fruit, killed, caught, or tamed, as many of the beasts, as he could; he that so imployed his pains about any of the spontaneous products of nature, as any way to alter them from the state which nature put them in, by placing any of his labour on them, did thereby acquire a propriety in them: but if they perished, in his possession, without their due use; if the fruits rotted, or the venison putrified, before he could spend it, he offended against the common law of nature, and was liable to be punished; he invaded his neighbour's share, for he had no right, farther than his use called for any of them, and they might serve to afford him conveniencies of life.

38 The same measures governed the possession of land too: whatsoever he tilled and reaped, laid up and made use of, before it spoiled, that was his peculiar right; whatsoever he enclosed, and could feed, and make use of, the cattle and product was also his. But if either the grass of his enclosure rotted on the ground, or the fruit of his planting perished without gathering, and laying up, this part of the earth, notwithstanding his enclosure, was still to be looked on as waste, and might be the possession of any other. Thus, at the beginning, Cain might take as much ground as he could till, and make it his own land, and yet leave enough to Abel's sheep to feed on; a few acres would serve for both their possessions. But as families increased, and industry inlarged their stocks, their possessions inlarged with the need of them; but yet it was commonly without any fixed property in the ground they made use of, till they incorporated, settled themselves together, and built cities; and then, by consent, they came in time, to set out the bounds of their distinct territories, and agree on limits between them and their neighbours; and by laws within themselves, settled the properties of those of the same society: for we see, that in that part of the world which was first inhabited, and therefore like to be best peopled, even as low down as Abraham's time, they wandered with their flocks, and their herds, which was their substance, freely up and down; and this Abraham did, in a country where he was a stranger. Whence it is plain, that at least a great part of the land lay in common; that the inhabitants valued it not, nor claimed property in any more than they made use of. But when there was not room enough in the same place, for their herds to feed together, they by consent, as Abraham and Lot did, Gen. xiii. 5. separated and inlarged their pasture, where it best liked them. And for the same reason Esau went from his father, and his brother, and planted in mount Seir, Gen. xxxvi. 6.

39 And thus, without supposing any private dominion, and property in Adam, over all the world, exclusive of all other men, which can no way be proved, nor any one's property be made out from it; but supposing the world given, as it was, to the children of men in common, we see how labour could make men distinct titles to several parcels of it, for their private uses; wherein there could be no doubt of right, no room for quarrel…

44 From all which it is evident, that though the things of nature are given in common, yet man, by being master of himself, and proprietor of his own person, and the actions or labour of it, had still in himself the great foundation of property; and that, which made up the great part of what he applied to the support or comfort of his being, when invention and arts had improved the convenien-cies of life, was perfectly his own, and did not belong in common to others.

SIX

Adam Smith

Adam Smith (1723 - 1790) was born in Scotland, presumably in the year 1723; there is no record of his birth but he was baptized June 5th 1723. Little is known about Smith's childhood and upbring except that his father died when he was still an infant. According to one of Smith's biographers he was abducted by Gypsies when he was four years old, and was rescued shortly thereafter.

Smith spend most of his life as a teacher. He taught at the University of Edinburgh, where he met and befriended David Hume, also a philosopher of great renown. Smith later taught at Glasgow University, but he resigned from the position to become the tutor of Henry Scott, Duke of Buccleuch. This position involved a great deal of travel, Smith toured Europe extensively as he followed his patron on his diplomatic business.

Smith is best known for his work, An Inquiry into the Nature and Causes of the Wealth of Nations, *often shortened to simply, the* Wealth of Nations. *In the excerpts included here Smith expounds upon the virtues of capitalism as an efficient and effective means of servicing the material needs of the populace. In the text Smith makes direct references to Locke, from whom he adopted the view that humans are naturally inclined to exercise their varied talents in the service of others. In the second excerpt Smith rebrands this inclination as a "propensity to truck, barter, and exchange one thing for another."*

Smith's Wealth of Nations
The Merits of Capitalism

Everybody must be sensible how much labour is facilitated and abridged by the application of proper machinery. It is unnecessary to give any example. I shall only observe, therefore, that the invention of all those machines by which labour is so much facilitated and abridged, seems to have been originally owing to the division of labour. Men are much more likely to discover easier and readier methods of attaining any object, when the whole attention of their minds is directed towards that single object, than when it is dissipated among a great variety of things. But, in consequence of the division of labour, the whole of every man's attention comes naturally to be directed towards some one very simple object. It is naturally to be expected, therefore, that some one or other of those who are employed in each particular branch of labour should soon find out easier and readier methods of performing their own particular work, whenever the nature of it admits of such improvement. A great part of the machines made use of in those manufactures in which labour is most subdivided, were originally the invention of common workmen, who, being each of them employed in some very simple operation, naturally turned their thoughts towards finding out easier and readier methods of performing it. Whoever has been much accustomed to visit such manufactures, must frequently have been shown very pretty machines, which were the inventions of such workmen, in order to facilitate and quicken their own particular part of the work. In the first fire engines {this was the current designation for steam engines}, a boy was constantly employed to open and shut alternately the communication between the boiler and the cylinder, according as the piston either ascended or descended. One of those boys, who loved to play with his companions, observed that, by tying a string from the handle of the valve which opened this communication to another part of the machine, the valve would open and shut without his assistance, and leave him at liberty to divert himself with his play-fellows. One of the greatest improvements that has been made upon this machine, since it was first invented, was in this manner the discovery of a boy who wanted to save his own labour.

All the improvements in machinery, however, have by no means been the inventions of those who had occasion to use the machines. Many improvements have been made by the ingenuity of the makers of the machines, when to make them became the business of a peculiar trade; and some by that of those who are called philosophers, or men of speculation, whose trade it is not to do any thing, but to observe every thing, and who, upon that account, are often capable of combining together the powers of the most distant and dissimilar objects in the progress of society, philosophy or speculation becomes, like every other employment, the principal or sole trade and occupation of a particular class of citizens. Like every other employment, too, it is subdivided into a great number of different branches, each of which affords occupation to a peculiar tribe or class of philosophers; and this subdivision of employment in philosophy, as well as in every other business, improve dexterity, and saves time. Each individual becomes more expert in his own peculiar branch, more work is done upon the whole, and the quantity of science is considerably increased by it.

It is the great multiplication of the productions of all the different arts, in consequence of the division of labour, which occasions, in a well-governed society, that universal opulence which extends itself to the lowest ranks of the people. Every workman has a great quantity of his own work to dispose of beyond what he himself has occasion for; and every other workman being exactly in the same situation, he is enabled to exchange a great quantity of his own goods for a great quantity or, what comes to the same thing, for the price of a great quantity of theirs. He supplies them abundantly with what they have occasion for, and they accommodate him as amply with what he has occasion for, and a general plenty diffuses itself through all the different ranks of the society.

Observe the accommodation of the most common artificer or day-labourer in a civilized and thriving country, and you will perceive that the number of people, of whose industry a part, though but a small part, has been employed in procuring him this accommodation, exceeds all computation. The woollen coat, for example, which covers the day-labourer, as coarse and rough as it may appear, is the produce of the joint labour of a great multitude of workmen. The shepherd, the sorter of the wool, the wool-comber or carder, the dyer, the scribbler, the spinner, the weaver, the fuller, the dresser, with many others, must all join their different arts in order to complete even this homely production. How many merchants and carriers, besides, must have been employed in transporting the materials from some of those workmen to others who often live in a very distant part of the country? How much commerce and navigation in particular, how many ship-builders, sailors, sail-makers, rope-makers, must have been employed in order to bring together the different drugs made use of by the dyer, which often come from the remotest corners of the world? What a variety of labour, too, is necessary in order to produce the tools of the meanest of those workmen! To say nothing of such complicated machines as the ship of the sailor, the mill of the fuller, or even the loom of the weaver, let us consider only what a variety of labour is requisite in order to form that very simple machine, the shears with which the shepherd clips the wool. The miner, the builder of the furnace for smelting the ore, the feller of the timber, the burner of the charcoal to be made use of in the smelting-house, the brick-maker, the bricklayer, the workmen who attend the furnace, the millwright, the forger, the smith, must all of them join their different arts in order to produce them. Were we to examine, in the same manner, all the different parts of his dress and household furniture, the coarse linen shirt which he wears next his skin, the shoes which cover his feet, the bed which he lies on, and all the different parts which compose it, the kitchen-grate at which he prepares his victuals, the coals which he makes use of for that purpose, dug from the bowels of the earth, and brought to him, perhaps, by a long sea and a long land-carriage, all the other utensils of his kitchen, all the furniture of his table, the knives and forks, the earthen or pewter plates upon which he serves up and divides his victuals, the different hands employed in preparing his bread and his beer, the glass window which lets in the heat and the light, and keeps out the wind and the rain, with all the knowledge and art requisite for preparing that beautiful and happy invention, without which these northern parts of the world could scarce have afforded a very comfortable habitation, together with the tools of all the different workmen employed in producing those different conveniencies; if we examine, I say, all these things, and consider what a variety of labour is employed about each of them, we shall be sensible that, without the assistance and co-operation of many thousands, the very meanest person in a civilized country could not be provided, even according to, what we very falsely imagine, the easy and simple manner in which he is commonly accommodated. Compared, indeed, with the more extravagant luxury of the great, his accommodation must no doubt appear extremely simple and easy; and yet it may be true, perhaps, that the accommodation of an European prince does not always so much exceed that of an industrious and frugal peasant, as the accommodation of the latter exceeds that of many an African king, the absolute masters of the lives and liberties of ten thousand naked savages.

Smith's Wealth of Nations
Human Propensity for Exchange

This division of labour, from which so many advantages are derived, is not originally the effect of any human wisdom, which foresees and intends that general opulence to which it gives occasion. It is the necessary, though very slow and gradual, consequence of a certain propensity in human nature, which has in view no such extensive utility; the propensity to truck, barter, and exchange one thing for another.

Whether this propensity be one of those original principles in human nature, of which no further account can be given, or whether, as seems more probable, it be the necessary consequence of the faculties of reason and speech, it belongs not to our present subject to inquire. It is common to all men, and to be found in no other race of animals, which seem to know neither this nor any other species of contracts. Two greyhounds, in running down the same hare, have sometimes the appearance of acting in some sort of concert. Each turns her towards his companion, or endeavours to intercept her when his companion turns her towards himself. This, however, is not the effect of any contract, but of the accidental concurrence of their passions in the same object at that particular time. Nobody ever saw a dog make a fair and deliberate exchange of one bone for another with another dog. Nobody ever saw one animal, by its gestures and natural cries signify to another, this is mine, that yours; I am willing to give this for that. When an animal wants to obtain something either of a man, or of another animal, it has no other means of persuasion, but to gain the favour of those whose service it requires. A puppy fawns upon its dam, and a spaniel endeavours, by a thousand attractions, to engage the attention of its master who is at dinner, when it wants to be fed by him. Man sometimes uses the same arts with his brethren, and when he has no other means of engaging them to act according to his inclinations, endeavours by every servile and fawning attention to obtain their good will. He has not time, however, to do this upon every occasion. In civilized society he stands at all times in need of the cooperation and assistance of great multitudes, while his whole life is scarce sufficient to gain the friendship of a few persons. In almost every other race of animals, each individual, when it is grown up to maturity, is entirely independent, and in its natural state has occasion for the assistance of no other living creature. But man has almost constant occasion for the help of his brethren, and it is in vain for him to expect it from their benevolence only. He will be more likely to prevail if he can interest their self-love in his favour, and shew them that it is for their own advantage to do for him what he requires of them. Whoever offers to another a bargain of any kind, proposes to do this. Give me that which I want, and you shall have this which you want, is the meaning of every such offer; and it is in this manner that we obtain from one another the far greater part of those good offices which we stand in need of. It is not from the benevolence of the butcher, the brewer, or the baker that we expect our dinner, but from their regard to their own interest. We address ourselves, not to their humanity, but to their self-love, and never talk to them of our own necessities, but of their advantages. Nobody but a beggar chooses to depend chiefly upon the benevolence of his fellow-citizens. Even a beggar does not depend upon it entirely. The charity of well-disposed people, indeed, supplies him with the whole fund of his subsistence. But though this principle ultimately provides him with all the necessaries of life which he has occasion for, it neither does nor can provide him with them as he has occasion for them. The greater part of his occasional wants are supplied in the same manner as those of other people, by treaty, by barter, and by purchase. With the money which one man gives him he purchases food. The old clothes which another bestows upon him he exchanges for other clothes which suit him better, or for lodging, or for food, or for money, with which he can buy either food, clothes, or lodging, as he has occasion.

As it is by treaty, by barter, and by purchase, that we obtain from one another the greater part of those mutual good offices which we stand in need of, so it is this same trucking disposition which originally gives occasion to the division of labour. In a tribe of hunters or shepherds, a particular person makes bows and arrows, for example, with more readiness and dexterity than any other. He frequently exchanges them for cattle or for venison, with his companions; and he finds at last that he can, in this manner, get more cattle and venison, than if he himself went to the field to catch them. From a regard to his own interest, therefore, the making of bows and arrows grows to be his chief business, and he becomes a sort of armourer. Another excels in making the frames and covers of their little huts or moveable houses. He is accustomed to be of use in this way to his neighbours, who reward him in the same manner with cattle and with venison, till at last he finds it his interest to dedicate himself entirely to this employment, and to become a sort of house-carpenter. In the same manner a third becomes a smith or a brazier; a fourth, a tanner or dresser of hides or skins, the principal part of the clothing of savages. And thus the certainty of being able to exchange all that surplus part of the produce of his own labour, which is over and above his own consumption, for such parts of the produce of other men's labour as he may have occasion for, encourages every man to apply himself to a particular occupation, and to cultivate and bring to perfection whatever talent of genius he may possess for that particular species of business.

The difference of natural talents in different men, is, in reality, much less than we are aware of; and the very different genius which appears to distinguish men of different professions, when grown up to maturity, is not upon many occasions so much the cause, as the effect of the division of labour. The difference between the most dissimilar characters, between a philosopher and a common street porter, for example, seems to arise not so much from nature, as from habit, custom, and education. When they came in to the world, and for the first six or eight years of their existence, they were, perhaps, very much alike, and neither their parents nor play-fellows could perceive any remarkable difference. About that age, or soon after, they come to be employed in very different occupations. The difference of talents comes then to be taken notice of, and widens by degrees, till at last the vanity of the philosopher is willing to acknowledge scarce any resemblance. But without the disposition to truck, barter, and exchange, every man must have procured to himself every necessary and conveniency of life which he wanted. All must have had the same duties to perform, and the same work to do, and there could have been no such difference of employment as could alone give occasion to any great difference of talents.

As it is this disposition which forms that difference of talents, so remarkable among men of different professions, so it is this same disposition which renders that difference useful. Many tribes of animals, acknowledged to be all of the same species, derive from nature a much more remarkable distinction of genius, than what, antecedent to custom and education, appears to take place among men. By nature a philosopher is not in genius and disposition half so different from a street porter, as a mastiff is from a grey-hound, or a grey-hound from a spaniel, or this last from a shepherd's dog. Those different tribes of animals, however, though all of the same species are of scarce any use to one another. The strength of the mastiff is not in the least supported either by the swiftness of the greyhound, or by the sagacity of the spaniel, or by the docility of the shepherd's dog. The effects of those different geniuses and talents, for want of the power or disposition to barter and exchange, cannot be brought into a common stock, and do not in the least contribute to the better accommodation and conveniency of the species. Each animal is still obliged to support and defend itself, separately and independently, and derives no sort of advantage from that variety of talents with which nature has distinguished its fellows. Among men, on the contrary, the most dissimilar geniuses are of use to one another; the different produces of their respective talents, by the general disposition to truck, barter, and exchange, being brought, as it were, into a common stock, where every man may purchase whatever part of the produce of other men's talents he has occasion for.

SEVEN

Immanuel Kant

Immanuel Kant (1724 - 1804) born in Königsberg, what was then the capital of Prussia and is today the city of Kaliningrad, located between Poland and Lithuania that is technically considered Russian territory. Kant apparently never travelled more than ten miles outside of Königsberg. His whole life, it would seem, was devoted to his studies.

Not surprisingly Kant became one of the pre-eminent theorists of all time. He wrote on metaphysics, epistemology, logic, the natural sciences, art, and jurisprudence, among other subjects. It is from Kant that we get our modern idea of 'genuis'--not in the sense that he exemplifies genius (which he does), but in the sense that it is Kant who first explains, in his work on art and the sublime, what it means to be a 'genius'. Of course, Kant also wrote on ethics, one of his main work on ethics being, The Groundwork of the Metaphysics of Morals, *more commonly referred to as the* Grundlagen, *the German word for "groundwork."*

In the selection from Groundwork *provided here, Kant opens his work, like Aristotle, with a statement of the central principle of analysis. Kant claims that the only thing that can correctly be called "good" without qualification of any sort is a good will. In what follows Kant unpacks this principle in order to arrive at the single principle that will guide the moral agent, possessed of a good will, to commit moral actions. For technical reasons, Kant refers to this principle as the "categorical imperative", and throughout the remainder of the text (in portions omitted from this collection) he will offer no less than four alternative articulations of the same principle. The statement of the categorical imperative that is the culmination of our excerpt has become an iconic slogan for ethical theorists.*

Kant's Groundwork
The Categorical Imperative

Nothing can possibly be conceived in the world, or even out of it, which can be called good, without qualification, except a good will. Intelligence, wit, judgement, and the other talents of the mind, however they may be named, or courage, resolution, perseverance, as qualities of temperament, are undoubtedly good and desirable in many respects; but these gifts of nature may also become extremely bad and mischievous if the will which is to make use of them, and which, therefore, constitutes what is called character, is not good. It is the same with the gifts of fortune. Power, riches, honour, even health, and the general well-being and contentment with one's condition which is called happiness, inspire pride, and often presumption, if there is not a good will to correct the influence of these on the mind, and with this also to rectify the whole principle of acting and adapt it to its end. The sight of a being who is not adorned with a single feature of a pure and good will, enjoying unbroken prosperity, can never give pleasure to an impartial rational spectator. Thus a good will appears to constitute the indispensable condition even of being worthy of happiness.

There are even some qualities which are of service to this good will itself and may facilitate its action, yet which have no intrinsic unconditional value, but always presuppose a good will, and this qualifies the esteem that we justly have for them and does not permit us to regard them as absolutely good. Moderation in the affections and passions, self-control, and calm deliberation are not only good in many respects, but even seem to constitute part of the intrinsic worth of the person; but they are far from deserving to be called good without qualification, although they have been so unconditionally praised by the ancients. For without the principles of a good will, they may become extremely bad, and the coolness of a villain not only makes him far more dangerous, but also directly makes him more abominable in our eyes than he would have been without it.

A good will is good not because of what it performs or effects, not by its aptness for the attainment of some proposed end, but simply by virtue of the volition; that is, it is good in itself, and considered by itself is to be esteemed much higher than all that can be brought about by it in favour of any inclination, nay even of the sum total of all inclinations. Even if it should happen that, owing to special disfavour of fortune, or the niggardly provision of a stepmotherly nature, this will should wholly lack power to accomplish its purpose, if with its greatest efforts it should yet achieve nothing, and there should remain only the good will (not, to be sure, a mere wish, but the summoning of all means in our power), then, like a jewel, it would still shine by its own light, as a thing which has its whole value in itself. Its usefulness or fruitlessness can neither add nor take away anything from this value. It would be, as it were, only the setting to enable us to handle it the more conveniently in common commerce, or to attract to it the attention of those who are not yet connoisseurs, but not to recommend it to true connoisseurs, or to determine its value.

There is, however, something so strange in this idea of the absolute value of the mere will, in which no account is taken of its utility, that notwithstanding the thorough assent of even common reason to the idea, yet a suspicion must arise that it may perhaps really be the product of mere high-flown fancy, and that we may have misunderstood the purpose of nature in assigning reason as the governor of our will. Therefore we will examine this idea from this point of view.

In the physical constitution of an organized being, that is, a being adapted suitably to the purposes of life, we assume it as a fundamental principle that no organ for any purpose will be found but what is also the fittest and best adapted for that purpose. Now in a being which has reason and a will, if the proper object of nature were its conservation, its welfare, in a word, its happiness, then nature would have hit upon a very bad arrangement in selecting the reason of the creature to carry out this purpose. For all the actions which the creature has to perform with a view to this purpose, and the whole rule of its conduct, would be far more surely prescribed to it by instinct, and that end would have been attained thereby much more certainly than it ever can be by reason. Should reason have been communicated to this favoured creature over and above, it must only have served it to contemplate the happy constitution of its nature, to admire it, to congratulate itself thereon, and to feel thankful for it to the beneficent cause, but not that it should subject its desires to that weak and delusive guidance and meddle bunglingly with the purpose of nature. In a word, nature would have taken care that reason should not break forth into practical exercise, nor have the presumption, with its weak insight, to think out for itself the plan of happiness, and of the means of attaining it. Nature would not only have taken on herself the choice of the ends, but also of the means, and with wise foresight would have entrusted both to instinct.

And, in fact, we find that the more a cultivated reason applies itself with deliberate purpose to the enjoyment of life and happiness, so much the more does the man fail of true satisfaction. And from this circumstance there arises in many, if they are candid enough to confess it, a certain degree of misology, that is, hatred of reason, especially in the case of those who are most experienced in the use of it, because after calculating all the advantages they derive, I do not say from the invention of all the arts of common luxury, but even from the sciences (which seem to them to be after all only a luxury of the understanding), they find that they have, in fact, only brought more trouble on their shoulders, rather than gained in happiness; and they end by envying, rather than despising, the more common stamp of men who keep closer to the guidance of mere instinct and do not allow their reason much influence on their conduct. And this we must admit, that the judgement of those who would very much lower the lofty eulogies of the advantages which reason gives us in regard to the happiness and satisfaction of life, or who would even reduce them below zero, is by no means morose or ungrateful to the goodness with which the world is governed, but that there lies at the root of these judgements the idea that our existence has a different and far nobler end, for which, and not for happiness, reason is properly intended, and which must, therefore, be regarded as the supreme condition to which the private ends of man must, for the most part, be postponed.

For as reason is not competent to guide the will with certainty in regard to its objects and the satisfaction of all our wants (which it to some extent even multiplies), this being an end to which an implanted instinct would have led with much greater certainty; and since, nevertheless, reason is imparted to us as a practical faculty, i.e., as one which is to have influence on the will, therefore, admitting that nature generally in the distribution of her capacities has adapted the means to the end, its true destination must be to produce a will, not merely good as a means to something else, but good in itself, for which reason was absolutely necessary. This will then, though not indeed the sole and complete good, must be the supreme good and the condition of every other, even of the desire of happiness. Under these circumstances, there is nothing inconsistent with the wisdom of nature in the fact that the cultivation of the reason, which is requisite for the first and unconditional purpose, does in many ways interfere, at least in this life, with the attainment of the second, which is always conditional, namely, happiness. Nay, it may even reduce it to nothing, without nature thereby failing of her purpose. For reason recognizes the establishment of a good will as its highest practical destination, and in attaining this purpose is capable only of a satisfaction of its own proper kind, namely that from the attainment of an end, which end again is determined by reason only, notwithstanding that this may involve many a disappointment to the ends of inclination.

We have then to develop the notion of a will which deserves to be highly esteemed for itself and is good without a view to anything further, a notion which exists already in the sound natural understanding, requiring rather to be cleared up than to be taught, and which in estimating the value of our actions always takes the first place and constitutes the condition of all the rest. In order to do this, we will take the notion of duty, which includes that of a good will, although implying certain subjective restrictions and hindrances. These, however, far from concealing it, or rendering it unrecognizable, rather bring it out by contrast and make it shine forth so much the brighter.

I omit here all actions which are already recognized as inconsistent with duty, although they may be useful for this or that purpose, for with these the question whether they are done from duty cannot arise at all, since they even conflict with it. I also set aside those actions which really conform to duty, but to which men have no direct inclination, performing them because they are impelled thereto by some other inclination. For in this case we can readily distinguish whether the action which agrees with duty is done from duty, or from a selfish view. It is much harder to make this distinction when the action accords with duty and the subject has besides a direct inclination to it. For example, it is always a matter of duty that a dealer should not over charge an inexperienced purchaser; and wherever there is much commerce the prudent tradesman does not overcharge, but keeps a fixed price for everyone, so that a child buys of him as well as any other. Men are thus honestly served; but this is not enough to make us believe that the tradesman has so acted from duty and from principles of honesty: his own advantage required it; it is out of the question in this case to suppose that he might besides have a direct inclination in favour of the buyers, so that, as it were, from love he should give no advantage to one over another. Accordingly the action was done neither from duty nor from direct inclination, but merely with a selfish view.

On the other hand, it is a duty to maintain one's life; and, in addition, everyone has also a direct inclination to do so. But on this account the of anxious care which most men take for it has no intrinsic worth, and their maxim has no moral import. They preserve their life as duty requires, no doubt, but not because duty requires. On the other band, if adversity and hopeless sorrow have completely taken away the relish for life; if the unfortunate one, strong in mind, indignant at his fate rather than desponding or dejected, wishes for death, and yet preserves his life without loving it- not from inclination or fear, but from duty- then his maxim has a moral worth.

To be beneficent when we can is a duty; and besides this, there are many minds so sympathetically constituted that, without any other motive of vanity or self-interest, they find a pleasure in spreading joy around them and can take delight in the satisfaction of others so far as it is their own work. But I maintain that in such a case an action of this kind, however proper, however amiable it may be, has nevertheless no true moral worth, but is on a level with other inclinations, e.g., the inclination to honour, which, if it is happily directed to that which is in fact of public utility and accordant with duty and consequently honourable, deserves praise and encouragement, but not esteem. For the maxim lacks the moral import, namely, that such actions be done from duty, not from inclination. Put the case that the mind of that philanthropist were clouded by sorrow of his own, extinguishing all sympathy with the lot of others, and that, while he still has the power to benefit others in distress, he is not touched by their trouble because he is absorbed with his own; and now suppose that he tears himself out of this dead insensibility, and performs the action without any inclination to it, but simply from duty, then first has his action its genuine moral worth. Further still; if nature has put little sympathy in the heart of this or that man; if he, supposed to be an upright man, is by temperament cold and indifferent to the sufferings of others, perhaps because in respect of his own he is provided with the special gift of patience and fortitude and supposes, or even requires, that others should have the same- and such a man would certainly not be the meanest product of nature- but if nature had not specially framed him for a philanthropist, would he not still find in himself a source from whence to give himself a far higher worth than that of a good-natured temperament could be? Unquestionably. It is just in this that the moral worth of the character is brought out which is incomparably the highest of all, namely, that he is beneficent, not from inclination, but from duty.

To secure one's own happiness is a duty, at least indirectly; for discontent with one's condition, under a pressure of many anxieties and amidst unsatisfied wants, might easily become a great temptation to transgression of duty. But here again, without looking to duty, all men have already the strongest and most intimate inclination to happiness, because it is just in this idea that all inclinations are combined in one total. But the precept of happiness is often of such a sort that it greatly interferes with some inclinations, and yet a man cannot form any definite and certain conception of the sum of satisfaction of all of them which is called happiness. It is not then to be wondered at that a single inclination, definite both as to what it promises and as to the time within which it can be gratified, is often able to overcome such a fluctuating idea, and that a gouty patient, for instance, can choose to enjoy what he likes, and to suffer what he may, since, according to his calculation, on this occasion at least, he has not sacrificed the enjoyment of the present moment to a possibly mistaken expectation of a happiness which is supposed to be found in health. But even in this case, if the general desire for happiness did not influence his will, and supposing that in his particular case health was not a necessary element in this calculation, there yet remains in this, as in all other cases, this law, namely, that he should promote his happiness not from inclination but from duty, and by this would his conduct first acquire true moral worth.

It is in this manner, undoubtedly, that we are to understand those passages of Scripture also in which we are commanded to love our neighbour, even our enemy. For love, as an affection, cannot be commanded, but beneficence for duty's sake may; even though we are not impelled to it by any inclination- nay, are even repelled by a natural and unconquerable aversion. This is practical love and not pathological- a love which is seated in the will, and not in the propensions of sense- in principles of action and not of tender sympathy; and it is this love alone which can be commanded.

The second proposition is: That an action done from duty derives its moral worth, not from the purpose which is to be attained by it, but from the maxim by which it is determined, and therefore does not depend on the realization of the object of the action, but merely on the principle of volition by which the action has taken place, without regard to any object of desire. It is clear from what precedes that the purposes which we may have in view in our actions, or their effects regarded as ends and springs of the will, cannot give to actions any unconditional or moral worth. In what, then, can their worth lie, if it is not to consist in the will and in reference to its expected effect? It cannot lie anywhere but in the principle of the will without regard to the ends which can be attained by the action. For the will stands between its a priori principle, which is formal, and its a posteriori spring, which is material, as between two roads, and as it must be determined by something, it that it must be determined by the formal principle of volition when an action is done from duty, in which case every material principle has been withdrawn from it.

The third proposition, which is a consequence of the two preceding, I would express thus Duty is the necessity of acting from respect for the law. I may have inclination for an object as the effect of my proposed action, but I cannot have respect for it, just for this reason, that it is an effect and not an energy of will. Similarly I cannot have respect for inclination, whether my own or another's; I can at most, if my own, approve it; if another's, sometimes even love it; i.e., look on it as favourable to my own interest. It is only what is connected with my will as a principle, by no means as an effect- what does not subserve my inclination, but overpowers it, or at least in case of choice excludes it from its calculation- in other words, simply the law of itself, which can be an object of respect, and hence a command. Now an action done from duty must wholly exclude the influence of inclination and with it every object of the will, so that nothing remains which can determine the will except objectively the law, and subjectively pure respect for this practical law, and consequently the maxim that I should follow this law even to the thwarting of all my inclinations.

Thus the moral worth of an action does not lie in the effect expected from it, nor in any principle of action which requires to borrow its motive from this expected effect. For all these effects- agreeableness of one's condition and even the promotion of the happiness of others- could have been also brought about by other causes, so that for this there would have been no need of the will of a rational being; whereas it is in this alone that the supreme and unconditional good can be found. The pre-eminent good which we call moral can therefore consist in nothing else than the conception of law in itself, which certainly is only possible in a rational being, in so far as this conception, and not the expected effect, determines the will. This is a good which is already present in the person who acts accordingly, and we have not to wait for it to appear first in the result.

But what sort of law can that be, the conception of which must determine the will, even without paying any regard to the effect expected from it, in order that this will may be called good absolutely and without qualification? As I have deprived the will of every impulse which could arise to it from obedience to any law, there remains nothing but the universal conformity of its actions to law in general, which alone is to serve the will as a principle, i.e., I am never to act otherwise than so that I could also will that my maxim should become a universal law. Here, now, it is the simple conformity to law in general, without assuming any particular law applicable to certain actions, that serves the will as its principle and must so serve it, if duty is not to be a vain delusion and a chimerical notion. The common reason of men in its practical judgements perfectly coincides with this and always has in view the principle here suggested. Let the question be, for example: May I when in distress make a promise with the intention not to keep it? I readily distinguish here between the two significations which the question may have: Whether it is prudent, or whether it is right, to make a false promise? The former may undoubtedly of be the case. I see clearly indeed that it is not enough to extricate myself from a present difficulty by means of this subterfuge, but it must be well considered whether there may not hereafter spring from this lie much greater inconvenience than that from which I now free myself, and as, with all my supposed cunning, the consequences cannot be so easily foreseen but that credit once lost may be much more injurious to me than any mischief which I seek to avoid at present, it should be considered whether it would not be more prudent to act herein according to a universal maxim and to make it a habit to promise nothing except with the intention of keeping it. But it is soon clear to me that such a maxim will still only be based on the fear of consequences. Now it is a wholly different thing to be truthful from duty and to be so from apprehension of injurious consequences. In the first case, the very notion of the action already implies a law for me; in the second case, I must first look about elsewhere to see what results may be combined with it which would affect myself. For to deviate from the principle of duty is beyond all doubt wicked; but to be unfaithful to my maxim of prudence may often be very advantageous to me, although to abide by it is certainly safer. The shortest way, however, and an unerring one, to discover the answer to this question whether a lying promise is consistent with duty, is to ask myself, "Should I be content that my maxim (to extricate myself from difficulty by a false promise) should hold good as a universal law, for myself as well as for others?" and should I be able to say to myself, "Every one may make a deceitful promise when he finds himself in a difficulty from which he cannot otherwise extricate himself?" Then I presently become aware that while I can will the lie, I can by no means will that lying should be a universal law. For with such a law there would be no promises at all, since it would be in vain to allege my intention in regard to my future actions to those who would not believe this allegation, or if they over hastily did so would pay me back in my own coin. Hence my maxim, as soon as it should be made a universal law, would necessarily destroy itself.

I do not, therefore, need any far-reaching penetration to discern what I have to do in order that my will may be morally good. Inexperienced in the course of the world, incapable of being prepared for all its contingencies, I only ask myself: Canst thou also will that thy maxim should be a universal law? If not, then it must be rejected, and that not because of a disadvantage accruing from it to myself or even to others, but because it cannot enter as a principle into a possible universal legislation, and reason extorts from me immediate respect for such legislation. I do not indeed as yet discern on what this respect is based (this the philosopher may inquire), but at least I understand this, that it is an estimation of the worth which far outweighs all worth of what is recommended by inclination, and that the necessity of acting from pure respect for the practical law is what constitutes duty, to which every other motive must give place, because it is the condition of a will being good in itself, and the worth of such a will is above everything.

Thus, then, without quitting the moral knowledge of common human reason, we have arrived at its principle. And although, no doubt, common men do not conceive it in such an abstract and universal form, yet they always have it really before their eyes and use it as the standard of their decision. Here it would be easy to show how, with this compass in hand, men are well able to distinguish, in every case that occurs, what is good, what bad, conformably to duty or inconsistent with it, if, without in the least teaching them anything new, we only, like Socrates, direct their attention to the principle they themselves employ; and that, therefore, we do not need science and philosophy to know what we should do to be honest and good, yea, even wise and virtuous. Indeed we might well have conjectured beforehand that the knowledge of what every man is bound to do, and therefore also to know, would be within the reach of every man, even the commonest. Here we cannot forbear admiration when we see how great an advantage the practical judgement has over the theoretical in the common understanding of men. In the latter, if common reason ventures to depart from the laws of experience and from the perceptions of the senses, it falls into mere inconceivabilities and self-contradictions, at least into a chaos of uncertainty, obscurity, and instability. But in the practical sphere it is just when the common understanding excludes all sensible springs from practical laws that its power of judgement begins to show itself to advantage. It then becomes even subtle, whether it be that it chicanes with its own conscience or with other claims respecting what is to be called right, or whether it desires for its own instruction to determine honestly the worth of actions; and, in the latter case, it may even have as good a hope of hitting the mark as any philosopher whatever can promise himself. Nay, it is almost more sure of doing so, because the philosopher cannot have any other principle, while he may easily perplex his judgement by a multitude of considerations foreign to the matter, and so turn aside from the right way. Would it not therefore be wiser in moral concerns to acquiesce in the judgement of common reason, or at most only to call in philosophy for the purpose of rendering the system of morals more complete and intelligible, and its rules more convenient for use (especially for disputation), but not so as to draw off the common understanding from its happy simplicity, or to bring it by means of philosophy into a new path of inquiry and instruction?

Innocence is indeed a glorious thing; only, on the other hand, it is very sad that it cannot well maintain itself and is easily seduced. On this account even wisdom- which otherwise consists more in conduct than in knowledge- yet has need of science, not in order to learn from it, but to secure for its precepts admission and permanence. Against all the commands of duty which reason represents to man as so deserving of respect, he feels in himself a powerful counterpoise in his wants and inclinations, the entire satisfaction of which he sums up under the name of happiness. Now reason issues its commands unyieldingly, without promising anything to the inclinations, and, as it were, with disregard and contempt for these claims, which are so impetuous, and at the same time so plausible, and which will not allow themselves to be suppressed by any command. Hence there arises a natural dialectic, i.e., a disposition, to argue against these strict laws of duty and to question their validity, or at least their purity and strictness; and, if possible, to make them more accordant with our wishes and inclinations, that is to say, to corrupt them at their very source, and entirely to destroy their worth- a thing which even common practical reason cannot ultimately call good.

Thus is the common reason of man compelled to go out of its sphere, and to take a step into the field of a practical philosophy, not to satisfy any speculative want (which never occurs to it as long as it is content to be mere sound reason), but even on practical grounds, in order to attain in it information and clear instruction respecting the source of its principle, and the correct determination of it in opposition to the maxims which are based on wants and inclinations, so that it may escape from the perplexity of opposite claims and not run the risk of losing all genuine moral principles through the equivocation into which it easily falls. Thus, when practical reason cultivates itself, there insensibly arises in it a dialectic which forces it to seek aid in philosophy, just as happens to it in its theoretic use; and in this case, therefore, as well as in the other, it will find rest nowhere but in a thorough critical examination of our reason.

EIGHT

Jeremy Bentham

Jeremy Bentham (1748 - 1832) was born to a wealthy and politically active London family. One of Bentham's earliest works was an essay critiquing the American Declaration of Independence published as part of John Lind's (An English lawyer, political activist and opponent of the American revolution) response to the Declaration. Bentham himself engaged in numerous political reform movements, including the policing and penal reform movements of his time.

Bentham was an influential contemporary of Adam Smith, leaders of the French Revolution, and James Mill, with whom he founded the controversial Westminster Review. *James Mill was also the father of John Stuart Mill, over whom Bentham will have a profound influence.*

Bentham is perhaps most famous for his posthumous attendance at University College London, where his remains are on public display decked out in his Sunday best a wooden cabinet.

In his Introduction to Principles of Morals and Legislation *Bentham offers the earliest and most comprehensive articulation of the tenets of utilitarianism. In our excerpt from the* Principles of Morals and Legislation *Bentham sets out his Hedonistic Calculus, a pseudo-mathematical scheme for determining which of any given number of potential responses to an ethical challenge is the most consistent with utilitarian ethics.*

Bentham's
Principles of Morals & Legislation
The Principle of Utility

I Nature has placed mankind under the governance of two sovereign masters, pain and pleasure. It is for them alone to point out what we ought to do, as well as to determine what we shall do. On the one hand the standard of right and wrong, on the other the chain of causes and effects, are fastened to their throne. They govern us in all we do, in all we say, in all we think: every effort we can make to throw off our subjection, will serve but to demonstrate and confirm it. In words a man may pretend to abjure their empire: but in reality he will remain. subject to it all the while. The principle of utility recognizes this subjection, and assumes it for the foundation of that system, the object of which is to rear the fabric of felicity by the hands of reason and of law. Systems which attempt to question it, deal in sounds instead of sense, in caprice instead of reason, in darkness instead of light.

But enough of metaphor and declamation: it is not by such means that moral science is to be improved.

II The principle of utility is the foundation of the present work: it will be proper therefore at the outset to give an explicit and determinate account of what is meant by it. By the principle of utility is meant that principle which approves or disapproves of every action whatsoever. according to the tendency it appears to have to augment or diminish the happiness of the party whose interest is in question: or, what is the same thing in other words to promote or to oppose that happiness. I say of every action whatsoever, and therefore not only of every action of a private individual, but of every measure of government.

III By utility is meant that property in any object, whereby it tends to produce benefit, advantage, pleasure, good, or happiness, (all this in the present case comes to the same thing) or (what comes again to the same thing) to prevent the happening of mischief, pain, evil, or unhappiness to the party whose interest is considered: if that party be the community in general, then the happiness of the community: if a particular individual, then the happiness of that individual.

IV The interest of the community is one of the most general expressions that can occur in the phraseology of morals: no wonder that the meaning of it is often lost. When it has a meaning, it is this. The community is a fictitious body, composed of the individual persons who are considered as constituting as it were its members. The interest of the community then is, what is it?—the sum of the interests of the several members who compose it.

V It is in vain to talk of the interest of the community, without understanding what is the interest of the individual. A thing is said to promote the interest, or to be for the interest, of an individual, when it tends to add to the sum total of his pleasures: or, what comes to the same thing, to diminish the sum total of his pains.

VI An action then may be said to be conformable to then principle of utility, or, for shortness sake, to utility, (meaning with respect to the community at large) when the tendency it has to augment the happiness of the community is greater than any it has to diminish it.

VII A measure of government (which is but a particular kind of action, performed by a particular person or persons) may be said to be conformable to or dictated by the principle of utility, when in like manner the tendency which it has to augment the happiness of the community is greater than any which it has to diminish it.

VIII When an action, or in particular a measure of government, is supposed by a man to be conformable to the principle of utility, it may be convenient, for the purposes of discourse, to imagine a kind of law or dictate, called a law or dictate of utility: and to speak of the action in question, as being conformable to such law or dictate.

IX A man may be said to be a partizan of the principle of utility' when the approbation or disapprobation he annexes to any action, or to any measure, is determined by and proportioned to the tendency which he conceives it to have to augment or to diminish the happiness of the community: or in other words, to its conformity or unconformity to the laws or dictates of utility.

X Of an action that is conformable to the principle of utility one may always say either that it is one that ought to be done, or at least that it is not one that ought not to be done. One may say also, that it is right it should be done; at least that it is not wrong it should be done: that it is a right action; at least that it is not a wrong action. When thus interpreted, the words ought, and right and wrong and others of that stamp, have a meaning: when otherwise, they have none.

XI Has the rectitude of this principle been ever formally contested? It should seem that it had, by those who have not known what they have been meaning. Is it susceptible of any direct proof? it should seem not: for that which is used to prove every thing else, cannot itself be proved: a chain of proofs must have their commencement somewhere. To give such proof is as impossible as it is needless.

XII Not that there is or ever has been that human creature at breathing, however stupid or perverse, who has not on many, perhaps on most occasions of his life, deferred to it. By the natural constitution of the human frame, on most occasions of their lives men in general embrace this principle, without thinking of it: if not for the ordering of their own actions, yet for the trying of their own actions, as well as of those of other men. There have been, at the same time, not many perhaps, even of the most intelligent, who have been disposed to embrace it purely and without reserve. There are even few who have not taken some occasion or other to quarrel with it, either on account of their not understanding always how to apply it, or on account of some prejudice or other which they were afraid to examine into, or could not bear to part with. For such is the stuff that man is made of: in principle and in practice, in a right track and in a wrong one, the rarest of all human qualities is consistency.

XIII When a man attempts to combat the principle of utility, it is with reasons drawn, without his being aware of it, from that very principle itself. His arguments, if they prove any thing, prove not that the principle is wrong, but that, according to the applications he supposes to be made of it, it is misapplied. Is it possible for a man to move the earth? Yes; but he must first find out another earth to stand upon.

XIV To disprove the propriety of it by arguments is impossible; but, from the causes that have been mentioned, or from some confused or partial view of it, a man may happen to be disposed not to relish it. Where this is the case, if he thinks the settling of his opinions on such a subject worth the trouble, let him take the following steps, and at length, perhaps, he may come to reconcile himself to it.

1. Let him settle with himself, whether he would wish to discard this principle altogether; if so, let him consider what it is that all his reasonings (in matters of politics especially) can amount to?
2. If he would, let him settle with himself, whether he would judge and act without any principle, or whether there is any other he would judge an act by?
3. If there be, let him examine and satisfy himself whether the principle he thinks he has found is really any separate intelligible principle; or whether it be not a mere principle in words, a kind of phrase, which at bottom expresses neither more nor less than the mere averment of his own unfounded sentiments; that is, what in another person he might be apt to call caprice?
4. If he is inclined to think that his own approbation or disapprobation, annexed to the idea of an act, without any regard to its consequences, is a sufficient foundation for him to judge and act upon, let him ask himself whether his sentiment is to be a standard of right and wrong, with respect to every other man, or whether every man's sentiment has the same privilege of being a standard to itself?
5. In the first case, let him ask himself whether his principle is not despotical, and hostile to all the rest of human race?
6. In the second case, whether it is not anarchial, and whether at this rate there are not as many different standards of right and wrong as there are men? and whether even to the same man, the same thing, which is right to-day, may not (without the least change in its nature) be wrong to-morrow? and whether the same thing is not right and wrong in the same place at the same time? and in either case, whether all argument is not at an end? and whether, when two men have said, "I like this", and "I don't like it", they can (upon such a principle) have any thing more to say?
7. If he should have said to himself, No: for that the sentiment which he proposes as a standard must be grounded on reflection, let him say on what particulars the reflection is to turn? if on particulars having relation to the utility of the act, then let him say whether this is not deserting his own principle, and borrowing assistance from that very one in opposition to which he sets it up: or if not on those particulars, on what other particulars?
8. If he should be for compounding the matter, and adopting his own principle in part, and the principle of utility in part, let him say how far he will adopt it?

9. When he has settled with himself where he will stop, then let him ask himself how he justifies to himself the adopting it so far? and why he will not adopt it any farther?

Admitting any other principle than the principle of utility to be a right principle, a principle that it is right for a man to pursue; admitting (what is not true) that the word right can have a meaning without reference to utility, let him say whether there is any such thing as a motive that a man can have to pursue the dictates of it: if there is, let him say what that motive is, and how it is to be distinguished from those which enforce the dictates of utility: if not, then lastly let him say what it is this other principle can be good for?

Bentham's
Principles of Morals & Legislation
Hedonistic Calculus

I Pleasures then, and the avoidance of pains, are the ends that the legislator has in view; it behoves him therefore to understand their value. Pleasures and pains are the instruments he has to work with: it behoves him therefore to understand their force, which is again, in other words, their value.

II To a person considered by himself, the value of a pleasure or pain considered by itself, will be greater or less, according to the four following circumstances:

1. Its intensity.
2. Its duration.
3. Its certainty or uncertainty.
4. Its propinquity or remoteness.

III These are the circumstances which are to be considered in estimating a pleasure or a pain considered each of them by itself. But when the value of any pleasure or pain is considered for the purpose of estimating the tendency of any act by which it is produced, there are two other circumstances to be taken into the account; these are,

5. Its fecundity, or the chance it has of being followed by sensations of the same kind: that is, pleasures, if it be a pleasure: pains, if it be a pain.
6. Its purity, or the chance it has of not being followed by sensations of the opposite kind: that is, pains, if it be a pleasure: pleasures, if it be a pain.

These two last, however, are in strictness scarcely to be deemed properties of the pleasure or the pain itself; they are not, therefore, in strictness to be taken into the account of the value of that pleasure or that pain. They are in strictness to be deemed properties only of the act, or other event, by which such pleasure or pain has been produced; and accordingly are only to be taken into the account of the tendency of such act or such event.

IV To a number of persons, with reference to each of whom to the value of a pleasure or a pain is considered, it will be greater or less, according to seven circumstances: to wit, the six preceding ones; viz.

1. Its intensity.
2. Its duration.
3. Its certainty or uncertainty.
4. Its propinquity or remoteness.
5. Its fecundity.
6. Its purity.

And one other; to wit:

7. Its extent; that is, the number of persons to whom it extends; or (in other words) who are affected by it.

V To take an exact account then of the general tendency of any act, by which the interests of a community are affected, proceed as follows. Begin with any one person of those whose interests seem most immediately to be affected by it: and take an account,

7. Of the value of each distinguishable pleasure which appears to be produced by it in the first instance.
8. Of the value of each pain which appears to be produced by it in the first instance.
9. Of the value of each pleasure which appears to be produced by it after the first. This constitutes the fecundity of the first pleasure and the impurity of the first pain.
10. Of the value of each pain which appears to be produced by it after the first. This constitutes the fecundity of the first pain, and the impurity of the first pleasure.
11. Sum up all the values of all the pleasures on the one side, and those of all the pains on the other. The balance, if it be on the side of pleasure, will give the good tendency of the act upon the whole, with respect to the interests of that individual person; if on the side of pain, the bad tendency of it upon the whole.
12. Take an account of the number of persons whose interests appear to be concerned; and repeat the above process with respect to each. Sum up the numbers expressive of the degrees of good tendency, which the act has, with respect to each individual, in regard to whom the tendency of it is good upon the whole: do this again with respect to each individual, in regard to whom the tendency of it is good upon the whole:

do this again with respect to each individual, in regard to whom the tendency of it is bad upon the whole. Take the balance which if on the side of pleasure, will give the general good tendency of the act, with respect to the total number or community of individuals concerned; if on the side of pain,the general evil tendency, with respect to the same community.

VI It is not to be expected that this process should be strictly pursued previously to every moral judgment, or to every legislative or judicial operation. It may, however, be always kept in view: and as near as the process actually pursued on these occasions approaches to it, so near will such process approach to the character of an exact one.

VII The same process is alike applicable to pleasure and pain' in whatever shape they appear: and by whatever denomination they are distinguished: to pleasure, whether it be called good (which is properly the cause or instrument of pleasure) or profit (which is distant pleasure, or the cause or instrument of, distant pleasure,) or convenience, or advantage, benefit, emolument, happiness, and so forth: to pain, whether it be called evil, (which corresponds to good) or mischief, or inconvenience. or disadvantage, or loss, or unhappiness, and so forth.

VIII Nor is this a novel and unwarranted, any more than it is a useless theory. In all this there is nothing but what the practice of mankind, wheresoever they have a clear view of their own interest, is perfectly conformable to. An article of property, an estate in land, for instance, is valuable, on what account? On account of the pleasures of all kinds which it enables a man to produce, and what comes to the same thing the pains of all kinds which it enables him to avert. But the value of such an article of property is universally understood to rise or fall according to the length or shortness of the time which a man has in it: the certainty or uncertainty of its coming into possession: and the nearness or remoteness of the time at which, if at all, it is to come into possession. As to the intensity of the pleasures which a man may derive from it, this is never thought of, because it depends upon the use which each particular person may come to make of it; which cannot be estimated till the particular pleasures he may come to derive from it, or the particular pains he may come to exclude by means of it, are brought to view. For the same reason, neither does he think of the fecundity or purity of those pleasures.

Thus much for pleasure and pain, happiness and unhappiness, in general. We come now to consider the several particular kinds of pain and pleasure.

NINE

Karl Marx

Karl Marx (1818 - 1883) is one of the privileged few philosophers to enjoy a popular readership outside of academia and philosophical circles. Marx was born in the Prussian town of Trier (which is now considered the oldest city in Germany). He was raised in a middle-class family before traveling to Bonn, where he began his studies. Always a rabble-rouser, Marx became involved in the Young Hegelians, a group of social critics influenced by G.W.F. Hegel (1770 - 1831). Later, having completed his schooling, Marx became a journalist writing for the radical newspaper the Rhineland News. *Marx later became the Co-Editor of the* German-French Annals, *another socialist newspaper. Eventually, Marx was no longer welcome in Prussia, and he was exiled from France because of his socialist publications. Marx spent the rest of his life working and writing in Brussels, Cologne, and London, where he died.*

Marx is most famous for his Das Kapital *or collaboration with Friedrich Engels (1820 - 1895) on* The Communist Manifesto. *However, the selection chosen for this anthology is from a speech delivered by Marx to the International Workingmen's Association published under the title, "Value, Price, and Profit". In our excerpt we find Marx revisiting the notion of the distribution of labour.*

Marx's "Value, Price, & Profit"

The Value of Labour

Citizens, I have now arrived at a point where I must enter upon the real development of the question. I cannot promise to do this in a very satisfactory way, because to do so I should be obliged to go over the whole field of political economy. I can, as the French would say, but "effleurer la question," touch upon the main points. The first question we have to put is: What is the value of a commodity? How is it determined?

At first sight it would seem that the value of a commodity is a thing quite relative, and not to be settled without considering one commodity in its relations to all other commodities. In fact, in speaking of the value, the value in exchange of a commodity, we mean the proportional quantities in which it exchanges with all other commodities. But then arises the question: How are the proportions in which commodities exchange with each other regulated? We know from experience that these proportions vary infinitely. Taking one single commodity, wheat, for instance, we shall find that a quarter of wheat exchanges in almost countless variations of proportion with different commodities. Yet, its value remaining always the same, whether expressed in silk, gold, or any other commodity, it must be something distinct from, and independent of, these different rates of exchange with different articles. It must be possible to express, in a very different form, these various equations with various commodities.

Besides, if I say a quarter of wheat exchanges with iron in a certain proportion, or the value of a quarter of wheat is expressed in a certain amount of iron, I say that the value of wheat and its equivalent in iron are equal to some third thing, which is neither wheat nor iron, because I suppose them to express the same magnitude in two different shapes. Either of them, the wheat or the iron, must, therefore, independently of the other, be reducible to this third thing which is their common measure.

To elucidate this point I shall recur to a very simple geometrical illustration. In comparing the areas of triangles of all possible forms and magnitudes, or comparing triangles with rectangles, or any other rectilinear figure, how do we proceed? We reduce the area of any triangle whatever to an expression quite different from its visible form. Having found from the nature of the triangle that its area is equal to half the product of its base by its height, we can then compare the different values of all sorts of triangles, and of all rectilinear figures whatever, because all of them may be resolved into a certain number of triangles.

The same mode of procedure must obtain with the values of commodities. We must be able to reduce all of them to an expression common to all, and distinguishing them only by the proportions in which they contain that identical measure.

As the exchangeable values of commodities are only social functions of those things, and have nothing at all to do with the natural qualities, we must first ask, What is the common social substance of all commodities? It is labour. To produce a commodity a certain amount of labour must be bestowed upon it, or worked up in it. And I say not only labour, but social labour. A man who produces an article for his own immediate use, to consume it himself, creates a product, but not a commodity. As a self-sustaining producer he has nothing to do with society. But to produce a commodity, a man must not only produce an article satisfying some social want, but his labour itself must form part and parcel of the total sum of labour expended by society. It must be subordinate to the division of labour within society. It is nothing without the other divisions of labour, and on its part is required to integrate them.

If we consider commodities as values, we consider them exclusively under the single aspect of realized, fixed, or, if you like, crystallized social labour. In this respect they can differ only by representing greater or smaller quantities of labour, as, for example, a greater amount of labour may be worked up in a silken handkerchief than in a brick. But how does one measure quantities of labour? By the time the labour lasts, in measuring the labour by the hour, the day, etc. Of course, to apply this measure, all sorts of labour are reduced to average or simple labour as their unit. We arrive, therefore, at this conclusion. A commodity has a value, because it is a crystallization of social labour. The greatness of its value, or its relative value, depends upon the greater or less amount of that social substance contained in it; that is to say, on the relative mass of labour necessary for its production. The relative values of commodities are, therefore, determined by the respective quantities or amounts of labour, worked up, realized, fixed in them. The correlative quantities of commodities which can be produced in the same time of labour are equal. Or the value of one commodity is to the value of another commodity as the quantity of labour fixed in the one is to the quantity of labour fixed in the other.

I suspect that many of you will ask, Does then, indeed, there exist such a vast of any difference whatever, between determining the values of commodities by wages, and determining them by the relative quantities of labour necessary for their production? You must, however, be aware that the reward for labour, and quantity of labour, are quite disparate things. Suppose, for example, equal quantities of labour to be fixed in one quarter of wheat and once ounce of gold. I resort to the example because it was used by Benjamin Franklin in his first Essay published in 1721, and entitled a modest enquiry into the nature and necessity of a paper currency, where he, one of the first, hit upon the true nature of value.

Well. We suppose, then, that one quarter of wheat and one ounce of gold are equal values or equivalents, because they are crystalizations of equal amounts of average labour, of so many days' or so many weeks' labour respectively fixed in them. In thus determining the relative values of gold and corn, do we refer in any way whatever to the wages of the agricultural labourer and the miner? Not a bit. We leave it quite indeterminate how their day's or their week's labour was paid, or even whether wages labour was employed at all. If it was, wages may have been very unequal. The labourer whose labour is realized in the quarter of wheat may receive two bushels only, and the labourer employed in mining may receive on-half of the ounce of gold. Or, supposing their wages to be equal, they may deviate in all possible proportions from the values of the commodities produced by them. They may amount to one-fourth, one-fifth, or any other proportional part of the one quarter of corn or the one ounce of gold. Their wages can, of course, not exceed, not be more than the values of the commodities they produced, by they can be less in every possible degree. Their wages will be limited by the values of the products, but the values of their products will not be limited by the wages. And above all, the values, the relative values of corn and gold, for example, will have been settled without any regard whatever to the value of the labour employed, that is to say, to wages. To determine the values of commodities by the relative quantities of labour fixed in them, is, therefore, a thing quite different from the tautological method of determining the values of commodities by the value of labour, or by wages. This point, however, will be further elucidated in the progress of our inquiry.

In calculating the exchangeable value of a commodity we must add to the quantity of labour previously worked up in the raw material of the commodity, and the labour bestowed on the implements, tools, machinery, and buildings, with which such labour is assisted. For example, the value of a certain amount of cotton yarn is the crystallization of the quantity of labour added to the cotton during the spinning process, the quantity of labour previously realized in the cotton itself, the quantity of labour realized in the coal, oil, and other auxiliary substances used, the quantity of labour fixed in the steam-engine, the spindles, the factory building, and so forth Instruments of production properly so-called, such as tools, machinery, buildings, serve again and again for longer or shorter period during repeated processes of production. If they were used up at once, like the raw material, their whole value would at once be transferred to the commodities they assist in producing. But as a spindle, for example, is but gradually used up, an average calculation is made, based upon the average time it lasts, and its average waste or wear and tear during a certain period, say a day. In this way we calculate how much of the value of the spindle is transferred to the yarn daily spin, and how much, therefore, of the total amount of labour realized in a pound of yarn, for example, is due to the quantity of labour previously realized in the spindle. For our present purpose it is not necessary to dwell any longer upon this point.

It might seem that if the value of a commodity is determined by the quantity of labour bestowed upon its production, the lazier a man, or the clumsier a man, the more valuable his commodity, because the greater the time of labour required for finishing the commodity. This, however, would be a sad mistake. You will recollect that I used the word "social labour," and many points are involved in this qualification of "social." In saying that the value of a commodity is determined by the quantity of labour worked up or crystalized in it, we mean the quantity of labour necessary for its production in a given state of society, under certain social average conditions of production, with a given social average intensity, and average skill of the labour employed. When, in England, the power-loom came to compete with the hand-loom, only half the former time of labour was wanted to convert a given amount of yarn into a yard of cotton or cloth. The poor hand-loom weaver now worked seventeen or eighteen hours daily, instead of the nine or the hours he had worked before. Still the product of twenty hours of his labour represented now only ten social hours of labour, or ten hours of labour socially necessary for the conversion of a certain amount of yarn into textile stuffs. His product of twenty hours had, therefore, no more value than his former product of ten hours.

If then the quantity of socially necessary labour realized in commodities regulates their exchangeable values, every increase in the quantity of labour wanted for the production of a commodity must augment its value, as every diminution must lower it.

If the respective quantities of labour necessary for the production of the respective commodities remained constant, their relative values also would be constant. But such is not the case. The quantity of labour necessary for the production of a commodity changes continuously with the changes in the productive powers of labour, the more produce is finished in a given time of labour; and the smaller the productive powers of labour, the less produce is finished in the same time. If, for example, in the progress of population it should become necessary to cultivate less fertile soils, the same amount of produce would be only attainable by a greater amount of labour spent, and the value of agricultural produce would consequently rise. On the other hand, if, with the modern means of production, a single spinner converts into yarn, during one working day, many thousand times the amount of cotton which he could have spun during the same time with the spinning wheel, it is evident that every single pound of cotton will absorb many thousand times less of spinning labour than it did before, and consequently, the value added by spinning to every single pound of cotton will be a thousand times less than before. The value of yarn will sink accordingly.

Apart from the different natural energies and acquired working abilities of different peoples, the productive powers of labour must principally depend: "”

Firstly. Upon the natural conditions of labour, such as fertility of soil, mines, and so forth.

Secondly. Upon the progressive improvement of the social powers of labour, such as are derived from production on a grand scale, concentration of capital and combination of labour, subdivision of labour, machinery, improved methods, appliance of chemical and other natural agencies, shortening of time and space by means of communication and transport, and every other contrivance by which science presses natural agencies into the service of labour, and by which the social or co-operative character of labour is developed. The greater the productive powers of labour, the less labour is bestowed upon a given amount of produce; hence the smaller the value of the produce. The smaller the productive powers of labour, the more labour is bestowed upon the same amount of produce; hence the greater its value. As a general law we may, therefore, set it down that: "”

The values of commodities are directly as the times of labour employed in their production, and are inversely as the productive powers of the labour employed.

Having till now only spoken of value, I shall add a few words about price, which is a peculiar from assumed by value.

Price, taken by itself, is nothing but the monetary expression of value. The values of all commodities of the country, for example, are expressed in gold prices, while on the Continent they are mainly expressed in silver prices. The value of gold or silver, like that of all other commodities is regulated by the quantity of labour necessary for getting them. You exchange a certain amount of your national products, in which a certain amount of your national labour is crystallized, for the produce of the gold and silver producing countries, in which a certain quantity of their labour is crystallized. It is in this way, in fact by barter, that you learn to express in gold and silver the values of all commodities, that is the respective quantities of labour bestowed upon them. Looking somewhat closer into the monetary expression of value, or what comes to the same, the conversion of value into price, you will find that it is a process by which you give to the values of all commodities an independent and homogeneous form, or by which you express them as quantities of equal social labour. So far as it is but the monetary expression of value, price has been called natural price by Adam Smith, "prix necessaire" by the French physiocrats. What then is the relation between value and market prices, or between natural prices and market prices? You all know that the market price is the same for all commodities of the same kind, however the conditions of production may differ for the individual producers. The market price expresses only the average amount of social labour necessary, under the average conditions of production, to supply the market with a certain mass of a certain article. It is calculated upon the whole lot of a commodity of a certain description.

So far the market price of a commodity coincides with its value. On the other hand, the oscillations of market prices, rising now over, sinking now under the value or natural price, depend upon the fluctuations of supply and demand. The deviations of market prices from values are continual, but as Adam Smith says:

"The natural price is the central price to which the prices of commodities are continually gravitating. Different accidents may sometimes keep them suspended a good deal above it, and sometimes force them down even somewhat below it. But whatever may be the obstacles which hinder them from settling in this center of repose and continuance, they are constantly tending towards it."

I cannot now sift this matter. It suffices to say the if supply and demand equilibrate each other, the market prices of commodities will correspond with their natural prices, that is to say with their values, as determined by the respective quantities of labour required for their production. But supply and demand must constantly tend to equilibrate each other, although they do so only by compensating one fluctuation by another, a rise by a fall, and vice versa. If instead of considering only the daily fluctuations you analyze the movement of market prices for longer periods, as Mr. Tooke, for example, has done in his History of Prices, you will find that the fluctuations of market prices, their deviations from values, their ups and downs, paralyze and compensate each other; so that apart from the effect of monopolies and some other modifications I must now pass by, all descriptions of commodities are, on average, sold at their respective values or natural prices. The average periods during which the fluctuations of market prices compensate each other are different for different kinds of commodities, because with one kind it is easier to adapt supply to demand than with the other.

If the, speaking broadly, and embracing somewhat longer periods, all descriptions of commodities sell at their respective values, it is nonsense to suppose that profit, not in individual cases; but that the constant and usual profits of different trades spring from the prices of commodities, or selling them at a price over and above their value. The absurdity of this notion becomes evident if it is generalized. What a man would constantly win as a seller he would constantly lose as a purchaser. It would not do to say that there are men who are buyers without being sellers, or consumers without being producers. What these people pay to the producers, they must first get from them for nothing. If a man first takes your money and afterwards returns that money in buying your commodities, you will never enrich yourselves by selling your commodities too dear to that same man. This sort of transaction might diminish a loss, but would never help in realizing a profit. To explain, therefore, the general nature of profits, you must start from the theorem that, on an average, commodities are sold at their real values, and that profits are derived from selling them at their values, that is, in proportion to the quantity of labour realized in them. If you cannot explain profit upon this supposition, you cannot explain it at all. This seems paradox and contrary to every-day observation. It is also paradox that the earth moves round the sun, and that water consists of two highly inflammable gases. Scientific truth is always paradox, if judged by every-day experience, which catches only the delusive appearance of things.

Marx's "Value, Price, & Profit"
Struggle Between Capital & Labour

Having shown that the periodical resistance on the part of the working men against a reduction of wages, and their periodical attempts at getting a rise of wages, are inseparable from the wages system, and dictated by the very fact of labour being assimilated to commodities, and therefore subject to the laws, regulating the general movement of prices; having furthermore, shown that a general rise of wages would result in a fall in the general rate of profit, but not affect the average prices of commodities, or their values, the question now ultimately arises, how far, in this incessant struggle between capital and labour, the latter is likely to prove successful.

I might answer by a generalization, and say that, as with all other commodities, so with labour, its market price will, in the long run, adapt itself to its value; that, therefore, despite all the ups and downs, and do what he may, the working man will, on an average, only receive the value of his labour, which resolves into the value of his labouring power, which is determined by the value of the necessaries required for its maintenance and reproduction, which value of necessaries finally is regulated by the quantity of labour wanted to produce them.

But there are some peculiar features which distinguish the value of the labouring power, or the value of labour, from the values of all other commodities. The value of the labouring power is formed by two elements -- the one merely physical, the other historical or social. Its ultimate limit is determined by the physical element, that is to say, to maintain and reproduce itself, to perpetuate its physical existence, the working class must receive the necessaries absolutely indispensable for living and multiplying. The value of those indispensable necessaries forms, therefore, the ultimate limit of the value of labour. On the other hand, the length of the working day is also limited by ultimate, although very elastic boundaries. Its ultimate limit is given by the physical force of the labouring man. If the daily exhaustion of his vital forces exceeds a certain degree, it cannot be exerted anew, day by day.

However, as I said, this limit is very elastic. A quick succession of unhealthy and short-lived generations will keep the labour market as well supplied as a series of vigorous and long-lived generations. Besides this mere physical element, the value of labour is in every country determined by a traditional standard of life. It is not mere physical life, but it is the satisfaction of certain wants springing from the social conditions in which people are placed and reared up. The English standard of life may be reduced to the Irish standard; the standard of life of a German peasant to that of a Livonian peasant. The important part which historical tradition and social habitude play in this respect, you may learn from Mr. Thornton's work on over-population, where he shows that the average wages in different agricultural districts of England still nowadays differ more or less according to the more or less favourable circumstances under which the districts have emerged from the state of serfdom.

This historical or social element, entering into the value of labour, may be expanded, or contracted, or altogether extinguished, so that nothing remains but the physical limit. During the time of the anti-Jacobin war, undertaken, as the incorrigible tax eater and sinecurist, old George Rose, used to say, to save the comforts of our holy religion from the inroads of the French infidels, the honest English farmers, so tenderly handled in a former chapter of ours, depressed the wages of the agricultural labourers even beneath that mere physical minimum, but made up by Poor Laws the remainder necessary for the physical perpetuation of the race. This was a glorious way to convert the wages labourer into a slave, and Shakespeare's proud yeoman into a pauper.

By comparing the standard wages or values of labour in different countries, and by comparing them in different historical epochs of the same country, you will find that the value of labour itself is not a fixed but a variable magnitude, even supposing the values of all other commodities to remain constant.

A similar comparison would prove that not only the market rates of profit change, but its average rates.

But as to profits, there exists no law which determines their minimum. We cannot say what is the ultimate limit of their decrease. And why cannot we fix that limit? Because, although we can fix the minimum of wages, we cannot fix their maximum.

We can only say that, the limits of the working day being given, the maximum of profit corresponds to the physical minimum of wages; and that wages being given, the maximum of profit corresponds to such a prolongation of the working day as is compatible with the physical forces of the labourer. The maximum of profit is therefore limited by the physical minimum of wages and the physical maximum of the working day. It is evident that between the two limits of the maximum rate of profit and immense scale of variations is possible. The fixation of its actual degree is only settled by the continuous struggle between capital and labour, the capitalist constantly tending to reduce wages to their physical minimum, and to extend the working day to its physical maximum, while the working man constantly presses in the opposite direction.

The matter resolves itself into a question of the respective powers of the combatants.

As to the limitation of the working day in England, as in all other countries, it has never been settled except by legislative interference. Without the working men's continuous pressure from without that interference would never have taken place. But at all events, the result was not to be attained by private settlement between the working men and the capitalists. This very necessity of general political action affords the proof that in its merely economical action capital is the stronger side.

As to the limits of the value of labour, its actual settlement always depends upon supply and demand, I mean the demand for labour on the part of capital, and the supply of labour by the working men. In colonial countries the law of supply and demand favours the working man. Hence the relatively high standard of wages in the United States. Capital may there try its utmost. It cannot prevent the labour market from being continuously emptied by the continuous conversion of wages labourers into independent, self-sustaining peasants. The position of a wages labourer is for a very large part of the American people but a probational state, which they are sure to leave within a longer or shorter term. To mend this colonial state of things the paternal British Government accepted for some time what is called the modern colonization theory, which consists in putting an artificial high price upon colonial land, in order to prevent the too quick conversion of the wages labourer into the independent peasant.

But let us now come to old civilized countries, in which capital domineers over the whole process of production. Take, for example, the rise in England of agricultural wages from 1849 to 1859. What was its consequence? The farmers could not, as our friend Weston would have advised them, raise the value of wheat, nor even its market prices. They had, on the contrary, to submit to their fall. But during these eleven years they introduced machinery of all sorts, adopted more scientific methods, converted part of arable land into pasture, increased the size of farms, and with this the scale of production, and by these and other processes diminishing the demand for labour by increasing its productive power, made the agricultural population again relatively redundant. This is the general method in which a reaction, quicker or slower, of capital against a rise of wages takes place in old, settled countries. Ricardo has justly remarked that machinery is in constant competition with labour, and can often be only introduced when the price of labour has reached a certain height, but the appliance of machinery is but one of the many methods for increasing the productive powers of labour. The very same development which makes common labour relatively redundant simplifies, on the other hand, skilled labour, and thus depreciates it.

The same law obtains in another form. With the development of the productive powers of labour the accumulation of capital will be accelerated, even despite a relatively high rate of wages. Hence, one might infer, as Adam Smith, in whose days modern industry was still in its infancy, did infer, that the accelerated accumulation of capital must turn the balance in favour of the working man, by securing a growing demand for his labour. From this same standpoint many contemporary writers have wondered that English capital having grown in that last twenty years so much quicker than English population, wages should not have been more enhanced. But simultaneously with the progress of accumulation there takes place a progressive change in the composition of capital. That part of the aggregate capital which consists of fixed capital, machinery, raw materials, means of production in all possible forms, progressively increases as compared with the other part of capital, which is laid out in wages or in the purchase of labour. This law has been stated in a more or less accurate manner by Mr. Barton, Ricardo, Sismondi, Professor Richard Jones, Professor Ramsey, Cherbuilliez, and others.

If the proportion of these two elements of capital was originally one to one, it will, in the progress of industry, become five to one, and so forth. If of a total capital of 600, 300 is laid out in instruments, raw materials, and so forth, and 300 in wages, the total capital wants only to be doubled to create a demand for 600 working men instead of for 300. But if of a capital of 600, 500 is laid out in machinery, materials, and so forth and 100 only in wages, the same capital must increase from 600 to 3,600 in order to create a demand for 600 workmen instead of 300. In the progress of industry the demand for labour keeps, therefore, no pace with the accumulation of capital. It will still increase, but increase in a constantly diminishing ratio as compared with the increase of capital.

These few hints will suffice to show that the very development of modern industry must progressively turn the scale in favour of the capitalist against the working man, and that consequently the general tendency of capitalistic production is not to raise, but to sink the average standard of wages, or to push the value of labour more or less to its minimum limit. Such being the tendency of things in this system, is this saying that the working class ought to renounce their resistance against the encroachments of capital, and abandon their attempts at making the best of the occasional chances for their temporary improvement? If they did, they would be degraded to one level mass of broken wretches past salvation. I think I have shown that their struggles for the standard of wages are incidents inseparable from the whole wages system, that in 99 cases out of 100 their efforts at raising wages are only efforts at maintaining the given value of labour, and that the necessity of debating their price with the capitalist is inherent to their condition of having to sell themselves as commodities. By cowardly giving way in their everyday conflict with capital, they would certainly disqualify themselves for the initiating of any larger movement.

At the same time, and quite apart form the general servitude involved in the wages system, the working class ought not to exaggerate to themselves the ultimate working of these everyday struggles. They ought not to forget that they are fighting with effects, but not with the causes of those effects; that they are retarding the downward movement, but not changing its direction; that they are applying palliatives, not curing the malady. They ought, therefore, not to be exclusively absorbed in these unavoidable guerilla fights incessantly springing up from the never ceasing encroachments of capital or changes of the market. They ought to understand that, with all the miseries it imposes upon them, the present system simultaneously engenders the material conditions and the social forms necessary for an economical reconstruction of society. Instead of the conservative motto, "A fair day's wage for a fair day's work!" they ought to inscribe on their banner the revolutionary watchword, "Abolition of the wages system!"

After this very long and, I fear, tedious exposition, which I was obliged to enter into to do some justice to the subject matter, I shall conclude by proposing the following resolutions:

Firstly. A general rise in the rate of wages would result in a fall of the general rate of profit, but, broadly speaking, not affect the prices of commodities.

Secondly. The general tendency of capitalist production is not to raise, but to sink the average standard of wages.

Thirdly. Trades Unions work well as centers of resistance against the encroachments of capital. They fail partially from an injudicious use of their power. The fail generally from limiting themselves to a guerilla war against the effects of the existing system, instead of simultaneously trying to change it, instead of using their organized forces as a lever for the final emancipation of the working class that is to say the ultimate abolition of the wages system.

TEN

John Stuart Mill

John Stuart Mill (1806 - 1873) was the son of James Mill. James, who was a close companion of Jeremy Bentham, raised his son John according to strict utilitarian precepts. It was their express goal to create a child of exceptional intellect who would, eventually, become a zealous proponent of utilitarianism. John did prove to be an exceptional intellect: his training in Greek began when he was just three years old and it is said that he was reading Greek classics, including Plato, by the age of eight.

Despite, or maybe because of, his intense scholarly training and aptitudes John suffered a severe emotional breakdown at the age of twenty, which was followed by a long period of depression. During his life Mill advocated for women's rights and served as a member of British Parliament for the City of Westminster. Mill died in 1873 in Avignon, France, where he had retired with his wife.

As it turns out, Mill did indeed become, perhaps not zealous, but one of the leading proponents of utilitarianism. Among his many works, Mill's On Liberty *and* Utilitarianism *are considered two of the seminal texts of the Utilitarian school of thought. In the excerpt included here, drawn from* Utilitarianism, *Mill offers his summary of the central tenets of his version of the philosophy--specifically, Mill defines the "principle of utility."*

Mill's Utilitarianism
A Defense of Utilitarianism

The creed which accepts as the foundation of morals, Utility, or the Greatest Happiness Principle, holds that actions are right in proportion as they tend to promote happiness, wrong as they tend to produce the reverse of happiness. By happiness is intended pleasure, and the absence of pain; by unhappiness, pain, and the privation of pleasure. To give a clear view of the moral standard set up by the theory, much more requires to be said; in particular, what things it includes in the ideas of pain and pleasure; and to what extent this is left an open question. But these supplementary explanations do not affect the theory of life on which this theory of morality is grounded- namely, that pleasure, and freedom from pain, are the only things desirable as ends; and that all desirable things (which are as numerous in the utilitarian as in any other scheme) are desirable either for the pleasure inherent in themselves, or as means to the promotion of pleasure and the prevention of pain...

According to the Greatest Happiness Principle, as above explained, the ultimate end, with reference to and for the sake of which all other things are desirable (whether we are considering our own good or that of other people), is an existence exempt as far as possible from pain, and as rich as possible in enjoyments, both in point of quantity and quality; the test of quality, and the rule for measuring it against quantity, being the preference felt by those who in their opportunities of experience, to which must be added their habits of self-consciousness and self-observation, are best furnished with the means of comparison. This, being, according to the utilitarian opinion, the end of human action, is necessarily also the standard of morality; which may accordingly be defined, the rules and precepts for human conduct, by the observance of which an existence such as has been described might be, to the greatest extent possible, secured to all mankind; and not to them only, but, so far as the nature of things admits, to the whole sentient creation...

Now there is absolutely no reason in the nature of things why an amount of mental culture sufficient to give an intelligent interest in these objects of contemplation, should not be the inheritance of every one born in a civilized country. As little is there an inherent necessity that any human being should be a selfish egotist, devoid of every feeling or care but those which centre in his own miserable individuality. Something far superior to this is sufficiently common even now, to give ample earnest of what the human species may be made. Genuine private affections and a sincere interest in the public good, are possible, though in unequal degrees, to every rightly brought up human being. In a world in which there is so much to interest, so much to enjoy, and so much also to correct and improve, every one who has this moderate amount of moral and intellectual requisites is capable of an existence which may be called enviable; and unless such a person, through bad laws, or subjection to the will of others, is denied the liberty to use the sources of happiness within his reach, he will not fail to find this enviable existence, if he escape the positive evils of life, the great sources of physical and mental suffering- such as indigence, disease, and the unkindness, worthlessness, or premature loss of objects of affection. The main stress of the problem lies, therefore, in the contest with these calamities, from which it is a rare good fortune entirely to escape; which, as things now are, cannot be obviated, and often cannot be in any material degree mitigated. Yet no one whose opinion deserves a moment's consideration can doubt that most of the great positive evils of the world are in themselves removable, and will, if human affairs continue to improve, be in the end reduced within narrow limits. Poverty, in any sense implying suffering, may be completely extinguished by the wisdom of society, combined with the good sense and providence of individuals. Even that most intractable of enemies, disease, may be indefinitely reduced in dimensions by good physical and moral education, and proper control of noxious influences; while the progress of science holds out a promise for the future of still more direct conquests over this detestable foe. And every advance in that direction relieves us from some, not only of the chances which cut short our own lives, but, what concerns us still more, which deprive us of those in whom our happiness is wrapped up. As for vicissitudes of fortune, and other disappointments connected with worldly circumstances, these are principally the effect either of gross imprudence, of ill-regulated desires, or of bad or imperfect social institutions.

All the grand sources, in short, of human suffering are in a great degree, many of them almost entirely, conquerable by human care and effort; and though their removal is grievously slow- though a long succession of generations will perish in the breach before the conquest is completed, and this world becomes all that, if will and knowledge were not wanting, it might easily be made- yet every mind sufficiently intelligent and generous to bear a part, however small and inconspicuous, in the endeavour, will draw a noble enjoyment from the contest itself, which he would not for any bribe in the form of selfish indulgence consent to be without.

And this leads to the true estimation of what is said by the objectors concerning the possibility, and the obligation, of learning to do without happiness. Unquestionably it is possible to do without happiness; it is done involuntarily by nineteen-twentieths of mankind, even in those parts of our present world which are least deep in barbarism; and it often has to be done voluntarily by the hero or the martyr, for the sake of something which he prizes more than his individual happiness. But this something, what is it, unless the happiness of others or some of the requisites of happiness? It is noble to be capable of resigning entirely one's own portion of happiness, or chances of it: but, after all, this self-sacrifice must be for some end; it is not its own end; and if we are told that its end is not happiness, but virtue, which is better than happiness, I ask, would the sacrifice be made if the hero or martyr did not believe that it would earn for others immunity from similar sacrifices? Would it be made if he thought that his renunciation of happiness for himself would produce no fruit for any of his fellow creatures, but to make their lot like his, and place them also in the condition of persons who have renounced happiness? All honour to those who can abnegate for themselves the personal enjoyment of life, when by such renunciation they contribute worthily to increase the amount of happiness in the world; but he who does it, or professes to do it, for any other purpose, is no more deserving of admiration than the ascetic mounted on his pillar. He may be an inspiriting proof of what men can do, but assuredly not an example of what they should.

Though it is only in a very imperfect state of the world's arrangements that any one can best serve the happiness of others by the absolute sacrifice of his own, yet so long as the world is in that imperfect state, I fully acknowledge that the readiness to make such a sacrifice is the highest virtue which can be found in man. I will add, that in this condition the world, paradoxical as the assertion may be, the conscious ability to do without happiness gives the best prospect of realizing, such happiness as is attainable. For nothing except that consciousness can raise a person above the chances of life, by making him feel that, let fate and fortune do their worst, they have not power to subdue him: which, once felt, frees him from excess of anxiety concerning the evils of life, and enables him, like many a Stoic in the worst times of the Roman Empire, to cultivate in tranquillity the sources of satisfaction accessible to him, without concerning himself about the uncertainty of their duration, any more than about their inevitable end.

Meanwhile, let utilitarians never cease to claim the morality of self devotion as a possession which belongs by as good a right to them, as either to the Stoic or to the Transcendentalist. The utilitarian morality does recognize in human beings the power of sacrificing their own greatest good for the good of others. It only refuses to admit that the sacrifice is itself a good. A sacrifice which does not increase, or tend to increase, the sum total of happiness, it considers as wasted. The only self-renunciation which it applauds, is devotion to the happiness, or to some of the means of happiness, of others; either of mankind collectively, or of individuals within the limits imposed by the collective interests of mankind.

I must again repeat, what the assailants of utilitarianism seldom have the justice to acknowledge, that the happiness which forms the utilitarian standard of what is right in conduct, is not the agent's own happiness, but that of all concerned. As between his own happiness and that of others, utilitarianism requires him to be as strictly impartial as a disinterested and benevolent spectator. In the golden rule of Jesus of Nazareth, we read the complete spirit of the ethics of utility. To do as you would be done by, and to love your neighbour as yourself, constitute the ideal perfection of utilitarian morality. As the means of making the nearest approach to this ideal, utility would enjoin, first, that laws and social arrangements should place the happiness, or (as speaking practically it may be called) the interest, of every individual, as nearly as possible in harmony with the interest of the whole; and secondly, that education and opinion, which have so vast a power over human character, should so use that power as to establish in the mind of every individual an indissoluble association between his own happiness and the good of the whole; especially between his own happiness and the practice of such modes of conduct, negative and positive, as regard for the universal happiness prescribes; so that not only he may be unable to conceive the possibility of happiness to himself, consistently with conduct opposed to the general good, but also that a direct impulse to promote the general good may be in every individual one of the habitual motives of action, and the sentiments connected therewith may fill a large and prominent place in every human being's sentient existence. If the, impugners of the utilitarian morality represented it to their own minds in this its, true character, I know not what recommendation possessed by any other morality they could possibly affirm to be wanting to it; what more beautiful or more exalted developments of human nature any other ethical system can be supposed to foster, or what springs of action, not accessible to the utilitarian, such systems rely on for giving effect to their mandates.

The objectors to utilitarianism cannot always be charged with representing it in a discreditable light. On the contrary, those among them who entertain anything like a just idea of its disinterested character, sometimes find fault with its standard as being too high for humanity. They say it is exacting too much to require that people shall always act from the inducement of promoting the general interests of society. But this is to mistake the very meaning of a standard of morals, and confound the rule of action with the motive of it. It is the business of ethics to tell us what are our duties, or by what test we may know them; but no system of ethics requires that the sole motive of all we do shall be a feeling of duty; on the contrary, ninety-nine hundredths of all our actions are done from other motives, and rightly so done, if the rule of duty does not condemn them. It is the more unjust to utilitarianism that this particular misapprehension should be made a ground of objection to it, inasmuch as utilitarian moralists have gone beyond almost all others in affirming that the motive has nothing to do with the morality of the action, though much with the worth of the agent. He who saves a fellow creature from drowning does what is morally right, whether his motive be duty, or the hope of being paid for his trouble; he who betrays the friend that trusts him, is guilty of a crime, even if his object be to serve another friend to whom he is under greater obligations.

But to speak only of actions done from the motive of duty, and in direct obedience to principle: it is a misapprehension of the utilitarian mode of thought, to conceive it as implying that people should fix their minds upon so wide a generality as the world, or society at large. The great majority of good actions are intended not for the benefit of the world, but for that of individuals, of which the good of the world is made up; and the thoughts of the most virtuous man need not on these occasions travel beyond the particular persons concerned, except so far as is necessary to assure himself that in benefiting them he is not violating the rights, that is, the legitimate and authorized expectations, of any one else. The multiplication of happiness is, according to the utilitarian ethics, the object of virtue: the occasions on which any person (except one in a thousand) has it in his power to do this on an extended scale, in other words to be a public benefactor, are but exceptional; and on these occasions alone is he called on to consider public utility; in every other case, private utility, the interest or happiness of some few persons, is all he has to attend to. Those alone the influence of whose actions extends to society in general, need concern themselves habitually about large an object. In the case of abstinences indeed- of things which people forbear to do from moral considerations, though the consequences in the particular case might be beneficial- it would be unworthy of an intelligent agent not to be consciously aware that the action is of a class which, if practiced generally, would be generally injurious, and that this is the ground of the obligation to abstain from it. The amount of regard for the public interest implied in this recognition, is no greater than is demanded by every system of morals, for they all enjoin to abstain from whatever is manifestly pernicious to society.

The same considerations dispose of another reproach against the doctrine of utility, founded on a still grosser misconception of the purpose of a standard of morality, and of the very meaning of the words right and wrong. It is often affirmed that utilitarianism renders men cold and unsympathizing; that it chills their moral feelings towards individuals; that it makes them regard only the dry and hard consideration of the consequences of actions, not taking into their moral estimate the qualities from which those actions emanate. If the assertion means that they do not allow their judgment respecting the rightness or wrongness of an action to be influenced by their opinion of the qualities of the person who does it, this is a complaint not against utilitarianism, but against having any standard of morality at all; for certainly no known ethical standard decides an action to be good or bad because it is done by a good or a bad man, still less because done by an amiable, a brave, or a benevolent man, or the contrary. These considerations are relevant, not to the estimation of actions, but of persons; and there is nothing in the utilitarian theory inconsistent with the fact that there are other things which interest us in persons besides the rightness and wrongness of their actions. The Stoics, indeed, with the paradoxical misuse of language which was part of their system, and by which they strove to raise themselves above all concern about anything but virtue, were fond of saying that he who has that has everything; that he, and only he, is rich, is beautiful, is a king. But no claim of this description is made for the virtuous man by the utilitarian doctrine. Utilitarians are quite aware that there are other desirable possessions and qualities besides virtue, and are perfectly willing to allow to all of them their full worth. They are also aware that a right action does not necessarily indicate a virtuous character, and that actions which are blamable, often proceed from qualities entitled to praise. When this is apparent in any particular case, it modifies their estimation, not certainly of the act, but of the agent. I grant that they are, notwithstanding, of opinion, that in the long run the best proof of a good character is good actions; and resolutely refuse to consider any mental disposition as good, of which the predominant tendency is to produce bad conduct. This makes them unpopular with many people; but it is an unpopularity which they must share with every one who regards the distinction between right and wrong in a serious light; and the reproach is not one which a conscientious utilitarian need be anxious to repel.

If no more be meant by the objection than that many utilitarians look on the morality of actions, as measured by the utilitarian standard, with too exclusive a regard, and do not lay sufficient stress upon the other beauties of character which go towards making a human being lovable or admirable, this may be admitted. Utilitarians who have cultivated their moral feelings, but not their sympathies nor their artistic perceptions, do fall into this mistake; and so do all other moralists under the same conditions. What can be said in excuse for other moralists is equally available for them, namely, that, if there is to be any error, it is better that it should be on that side. As a matter of fact, we may affirm that among utilitarians as among adherents of other systems, there is every imaginable degree of rigidity and of laxity in the application of their standard: some are even puritanically rigorous, while others are as indulgent as can possibly be desired by sinner or by sentimentalist. But on the whole, a doctrine which brings prominently forward the interest that mankind have in the repression and prevention of conduct which violates the moral law, is likely to be inferior to no other in turning the sanctions of opinion again such violations. It is true, the question, What does violate the moral law? is one on which those who recognize different standards of morality are likely now and then to differ. But difference of opinion on moral questions was not first introduced into the world by utilitarianism, while that doctrine does supply, if not always an easy, at all events a tangible and intelligible mode of deciding such differences.

It may not be superfluous to notice a few more of the common misapprehensions of utilitarian ethics, even those which are so obvious and gross that it might appear impossible for any person of candour and intelligence to fall into them; since persons, even of considerable mental endowments, often give themselves so little trouble to understand the bearings of any opinion against which they entertain a prejudice, and men are in general so little conscious of this voluntary ignorance as a defect, that the vulgarest misunderstandings of ethical doctrines are continually met with in the deliberate writings of persons of the greatest pretensions both to high principle and to philosophy. We not uncommonly hear the doctrine of utility inveighed against as a godless doctrine. If it be necessary to say anything at all against so mere an assumption, we may say that the question depends upon what idea we have formed of the moral character of the Deity. If it be a true belief that God desires, above all things, the happiness of his creatures, and that this was his purpose in their creation, utility is not only not a godless doctrine, but more profoundly religious than any other. If it be meant that utilitarianism does not recognize the revealed will of God as the supreme law of morals, I answer, that a utilitarian who believes in the perfect goodness and wisdom of God, necessarily believes that whatever God has thought fit to reveal on the subject of morals, must fulfill the requirements of utility in a supreme degree. But others besides utilitarians have been of opinion that the Christian revelation was intended, and is fitted, to inform the hearts and minds of mankind with a spirit which should enable them to find for themselves what is right, and incline them to do it when found, rather than to tell them, except in a very general way, what it is; and that we need a doctrine of ethics, carefully followed out, to interpret to us the will God. Whether this opinion is correct or not, it is superfluous here to discuss; since whatever aid religion, either natural or revealed, can afford to ethical investigation, is as open to the utilitarian moralist as to any other. He can use it as the testimony of God to the usefulness or hurtfulness of any given course of action, by as good a right as others can use it for the indication of a transcendental law, having no connection with usefulness or with happiness.

Again, Utility is often summarily stigmatized as an immoral doctrine by giving it the name of Expediency, and taking advantage of the popular use of that term to contrast it with Principle. But the Expedient, in the sense in which it is opposed to the Right, generally means that which is expedient for the particular interest of the agent himself; as when a minister sacrifices the interests of his country to keep himself in place. When it means anything better than this, it means that which is expedient for some immediate object, some temporary purpose, but which violates a rule whose observance is expedient in a much higher degree. The Expedient, in this sense, instead of being the same thing with the useful, is a branch of the hurtful. Thus, it would often be expedient, for the purpose of getting over some momentary embarrassment, or attaining some object immediately useful to ourselves or others, to tell a lie. But inasmuch as the cultivation in ourselves of a sensitive feeling on the subject of veracity, is one of the most useful, and the enfeeblement of that feeling one of the most hurtful, things to which our conduct can be instrumental; and inasmuch as any, even unintentional, deviation from truth, does that much towards weakening the trustworthiness of human assertion, which is not only the principal support of all present social well-being, but the insufficiency of which does more than any one thing that can be named to keep back civilization, virtue, everything on which human happiness on the largest scale depends; we feel that the violation, for a present advantage, of a rule of such transcendent expediency, is not expedient, and that he who, for the sake of a convenience to himself or to some other individual, does what depends on him to deprive mankind of the good, and inflict upon them the evil, involved in the greater or less reliance which they can place in each other's word, acts the part of one of their worst enemies. Yet that even this rule, sacred as it is, admits of possible exceptions, is acknowledged by all moralists; the chief of which is when the withholding of some fact (as of information from a malefactor, or of bad news from a person dangerously ill) would save an individual (especially an individual other than oneself) from great and unmerited evil, and when the withholding can only be effected by denial. But in order that the exception may not extend itself beyond the need, and may have the least possible effect in weakening reliance on veracity, it ought to be recognized, and, if possible, its limits defined; and if the principle of utility is good for anything, it must be good for weighing these conflicting utilities against one another, and marking out the region within which one or the other preponderates.

Again, defenders of utility often find themselves called upon to reply to such objections as this- that there is not time, previous to action, for calculating and weighing the effects of any line of conduct on the general happiness. This is exactly as if any one were to say that it is impossible to guide our conduct by Christianity, because there is not time, on every occasion on which anything has to be done, to read through the Old and New Testaments. The answer to the objection is, that there has been ample time, namely, the whole past duration of the human species. During all that time, mankind have been learning by experience the tendencies of actions; on which experience all the prudence, as well as all the morality of life, are dependent. People talk as if the commencement of this course of experience had hitherto been put off, and as if, at the moment when some man feels tempted to meddle with the property or life of another, he had to begin considering for the first time whether murder and theft are injurious to human happiness. Even then I do not think that he would find the question very puzzling; but, at all events, the matter is now done to his hand.

It is truly a whimsical supposition that, if mankind were agreed in considering utility to be the test of morality, they would remain without any agreement as to what is useful, and would take no measures for having their notions on the subject taught to the young, and enforced by law and opinion. There is no difficulty in proving any ethical standard whatever to work ill, if we suppose universal idiocy to be conjoined with it; but on any hypothesis short of that, mankind must by this time have acquired positive beliefs as to the effects of some actions on their happiness; and the beliefs which have thus come down are the rules of morality for the multitude, and for the philosopher until he has succeeded in finding better. That philosophers might easily do this, even now, on many subjects; that the received code of ethics is by no means of divine right; and that mankind have still much to learn as to the effects of actions on the general happiness, I admit, or rather, earnestly maintain. The corollaries from the principle of utility, like the precepts of every practical art, admit of indefinite improvement, and, in a progressive state of the human mind, their improvement is perpetually going on.

But to consider the rules of morality as improvable, is one thing; to pass over the intermediate generalizations entirely, and endeavour to test each individual action directly by the first principle, is another. It is a strange notion that the acknowledgment of a first principle is inconsistent with the admission of secondary ones. To inform a traveller respecting the place of his. ultimate destination, is not to forbid the use of landmarks and direction-posts on the way. The proposition that happiness is the end and aim of morality, does not mean that no road ought to be laid down to that goal, or that persons going thither should not be advised to take one direction rather than another. Men really ought to leave off talking a kind of nonsense on this subject, which they would neither talk nor listen to on other matters of practical concernment. Nobody argues that the art of navigation is not founded on astronomy, because sailors cannot wait to calculate the Nautical Almanack. Being rational creatures, they go to sea with it ready calculated; and all rational creatures go out upon the sea of life with their minds made up on the common questions of right and wrong, as well as on many of the far more difficult questions of wise and foolish. And this, as long as foresight is a human quality, it is to be presumed they will continue to do. Whatever we adopt as the fundamental principle of morality, we require subordinate principles to apply it by; the impossibility of doing without them, being common to all systems, can afford no argument against any one in particular; but gravely to argue as if no such secondary principles could be had, and as if mankind had remained till now, and always must remain, without drawing any general conclusions from the experience of human life, is as high a pitch, I think, as absurdity has ever reached in philosophical controversy.

The remainder of the stock arguments against utilitarianism mostly consist in laying to its charge the common infirmities of human nature, and the general difficulties which embarrass conscientious persons in shaping their course through life. We are told that a utilitarian will be apt to make his own particular case an exception to moral rules, and, when under temptation, will see a utility in the breach of a rule, greater than he will see in its observance. But is utility the only creed which is able to furnish us with excuses for evil doing, and means of cheating our own conscience? They are afforded in abundance by all doctrines which recognize as a fact in morals the existence of conflicting considerations; which all doctrines do, that have been believed by sane persons. It is not the fault of any creed, but of the complicated nature of human affairs, that rules of conduct cannot be so framed as to require no exceptions, and that hardly any kind of action can safely be laid down as either always obligatory or always condemnable. There is no ethical creed which does not temper the rigidity of its laws, by giving a certain latitude, under the moral responsibility of the agent, for accommodation to peculiarities of circumstances; and under every creed, at the opening thus made, self-deception and dishonest casuistry get in. There exists no moral system under which there do not arise unequivocal cases of conflicting obligation. These are the real difficulties, the knotty points both in the theory of ethics, and in the conscientious guidance of personal conduct. They are overcome practically, with greater or with less success, according to the intellect and virtue of the individual; but it can hardly be pretended that any one will be the less qualified for dealing with them, from possessing an ultimate standard to which conflicting rights and duties can be referred. If utility is the ultimate source of moral obligations, utility may be invoked to decide between them when their demands are incompatible. Though the application of the standard may be difficult, it is better than none at all: while in other systems, the moral laws all claiming independent authority, there is no common umpire entitled to interfere between them; their claims to precedence one over another rest on little better than sophistry, and unless determined, as they generally are, by the unacknowledged influence of considerations of utility, afford a free scope for the action of personal desires and partialities. We must remember that only in these cases of conflict between secondary principles is it requisite that first principles should be appealed to. There is no case of moral obligation in which some secondary principle is not involved; and if only one, there can seldom be any real doubt which one it is, in the mind of any person by whom the principle itself is recognized.

Bibliography

Aquinas, St. Thomas. *The Summa Theologica.* Translated by Fathers of the English Dominican Province (Benziger Bros. Edition, 1947).

Aristotle. *Nicomachean Ethics*. Translated by W.D. Ross (Oxford: Clarendon Press, 1908).

Bentham, Jeremy. *Introduction to Principles of Morals and Legislation*. (Oxford: Clarendon Press, 1907).

Hobbes, Thomas. *Leviathan or The Matter, Forme and Power of a Common Wealth Ecclesiasticall and Civil*. (Andrew Crooke, 1651).

Kant, Immanuel. *Fundamental Principles of the Metaphysics of Ethics*. Translated by Thomas Kingsmill Abbot (Longmans, Green and Co., 1895).

Locke, John. *Two Treatises of Civil Government*. Edited by Thomas Hollis (A. Millar et al., 1764).

Marx, Karl. *Value, Price, & Profit*. (International Co., Inc, 1969).

Mill, John Stuart. *Utilitarianism*. Reprinted from *Fraser's Magazine* (Longmans, Green and Co., 1879).

Plato. *Euthyphro*. Translated by Benjamin Jowett in *The Dialogues of Plato, Volume 2.* (Oxford University Press, 1892).

——Republic. Translated by Benjamin Jowett in *The Dialogues of Plato, Volume 3.* (Oxford University Press,

Smith, Adam. *An Inquiry into the Nature and Causes of the Wealth of Nations*. Edited by Edwin Cannan (Methuen, 1904).

CPSIA information can be obtained at www.ICGtesting.com
Printed in the USA
LVOW01s0717140114

369245LV00007B/28/P

9 780988 119512